MARGIN OF EXCELLENCE

Margin of Excellence: The New Work of Higher Education Foundations

Library of Congress Cataloging-in-Publication Data

Margin of excellence : the new work of higher education foundations / Richard D. Legon, editor.
    p. cm.
Includes index.
    ISBN 0-9754948-1-3
    1. Educational fund raising — United States. 2. Public universities — United States — Finance. 3. Charitable uses, trusts, and foundations — United States. I. Legon, Richard D.
LB2335.95.M37 2005
378.1'06 — dc22

2005028250

For more information on AGB Publications or to order additional copies of this book, call 800/356-6317 or visit our web site at *www.agb.org*.

MARGIN OF EXCELLENCE

The **New Work**
of Higher Education Foundations

Richard D. Legon, Editor

**Association of Governing Boards
of Universities and Colleges**
One Dupont Circle • Suite 400
Washington, D.C. 20036

Margin of Excellence
THE NEW WORK OF HIGHER EDUCATION FOUNDATIONS

CONTENTS

Foreword

The publication of *Margin of Excellence: The New Work of Higher Education Foundations* represents another milestone in AGB's efforts to provide tools and services for the foundations affiliated with public higher education institutions and systems. This segment of AGB's membership — some 165 strong as of this writing — has become increasingly significant in the realm of public higher education.

Building on the success of the 1997 AGB book, *College and University Foundations: Serving America's Public Higher Education,* Richard D. Legon, editor and contributing author, has shaped this new volume to place foundations squarely in an environment that has experienced nothing less than a "sea change" resulting from a decade's potent mix of societal and financial forces.

Through its chapters covering innovative thinking, adaptability, and the development of effective and responsive board committees, *Margin of Excellence* reaches past its predecessor to equip foundation executives, boards, and the leaders of host institutions with the knowledge they need to strategically manage change and growth. Its focus on the essential elements of board composition, practice, and policy will help foundations of all types and sizes in their quest to effectively serve their institutions and public higher education.

This book challenges us to think differently, expansively, and more ambitiously about the possible — by avoiding complacency, by reaching for higher levels of achievement, and by participating more fully in the public-policy debates yet to come. Some of these debates will directly affect the ability of foundation executives and boards to do their jobs; others will concern matters that affect the condition and future of their host universities. It is a time for vigilance and action.

Of course, the real beneficiaries of AGB's partnership with the leaders of these foundations are the more than 12 million students who attend public colleges and universities nationwide — a figure that comprises 80 percent of the total enrollment in American higher education. We know that the capacity of public higher education to fulfill its mission depends increasingly on the ability of foundations to carry out their missions. That is why this book is so important. It is the only resource available that "drills down" into the essentials of "the new work" of foundations and their boards of directors and trustees.

The larger questions, as always, remain on the table. We are accustomed to reading explicit warnings that the United States must work harder to sustain its competitive edge in the changing and challenging international marketplace. No longer can we take success for granted. Foundations affiliated with public higher education institutions and systems — and the governing boards responsible for their success — will continue to be an essential determinant of the strength of American higher education.

RICHARD T. INGRAM
President
Association of Governing Boards
of Universities and Colleges
Washington, D.C.

viii

Preface

When AGB published the first guide for the boards of institutionally related foundations in 1997, there was already a long and important history of these separately incorporated organizations working in support of the nation's public colleges and universities. Since then, these foundations and their boards have witnessed the expectations placed on them change and grow. Fiscal challenges in the states intensified the pressure on foundations to attract private support for their host institutions and to manage assets wisely for the benefit of current and future generations of students. Currently, more than 1,500 foundations serve public higher education, a figure that includes the growing sector of community college foundations.

The record shows that foundation assets grew dramatically in response to the bull market of the late 1990s. And while the ensuing bear market caused a downturn for many foundation portfolios, the key role of foundations in helping to ensure a long-term future for public colleges and universities was never in doubt. The market's subsequent rebound has been an important element of current public institution funding.

This second AGB guide for foundation boards takes a thorough look at some of the emerging issues facing foundations — and through them the challenges confronting public higher education. It also provides a glimpse of how those issues are likely to affect the work of foundations over the next few years. Our purpose is not to gaze into a crystal ball but rather to connect recent trends in such areas as state funding for public higher education and increasing demands for accountability and transparency for boards, donors, and volunteers. Overall, *Margin of Excellence* aims to provide foundation directors, staff, and institutional leaders with an updated portrayal of their heightened responsibilities and how they are shaping changes in the governance of these increasingly complex organizations.

The contributing authors of *Margin of Excellence* bring formidable knowledge and experience to the discussion. The volume opens with an overview of the issues that have captured the attention of foundations today and that almost certainly will continue to challenge them in the coming years. Some of the ensuing chapters offer new perspectives on issues the first guide addressed; other chapters, such as Tom Roha's examination of foundation autonomy versus interdependence, discuss new or emerging themes. Building on his 2000 AGB Public Policy Paper, "University-Related Foundations and the Issue of Independence," Roha, a partner in the law firm of Roha and Flaherty in Washington, D.C., revisits the issues foundations face concerning the requirements necessary to meet standards of autonomy, as defined by some recent court decisions and state laws. These court cases and legislation will have a significant impact on how institutionally related foundations raise funds and manage donor relations and records.

More than half of this volume is dedicated to highlighting best practices in the work of foundation board committees. AGB has long advocated that the primary work of an effective board be conducted within its standing committees or in ad hoc committees and task forces that have a focused (and limited) charge. The chapters of *Margin of Excellence* devoted to committee work provide an overview of the most common standing committees of foundation boards and examine how various strategic challenges confronting foundations might affect the work of these committees. These chapters also offer committee members sample questions to consider.

It is an article of faith that boards should respect the expertise of each committee and entrust its members to carry out the committee's responsibilities with appropriate due diligence. Additionally, while it is useful to rotate directors periodically among committees to provide them with a broad understanding, each committee typically requires some degree of continuity and expertise to sustain high levels of performance. This is critically important for both the finance and investment committees, here addressed respectively by Marcia Muller, president of Wright State University Foundation, and John Griswold, executive director of Commonfund Institute.

AGB president Tom Ingram takes a detailed look at the importance of a foundation board's executive committee and calls on boards to assign essential responsibilities to that committee while maintaining the involvement of the full board on key policy issues.

Jim Lanier, president emeritus of the East Carolina University Foundation, and E.B. Wilson, board chair emeritus of St. Lawrence University, outline the overarching responsibilities of the committee on directors. Much of the board's structure and performance depends upon the effectiveness of this committee, and Lanier and Wilson's informative chapter looks at how the committee on directors can enhance the board's overall effectiveness and the performance of its members.

Royster Hedgepeth, a well-respected practitioner and student of foundation governance, calls for development committees to become more active in the foundation's fund-raising efforts. He offers checklists to help these committees effectively measure their performance.

Other board committees also might look at whether their responsibilities allow for a more strategic approach to their work. Linking committee agendas to the foundation's strategic plan enables the board to process its work effectively while facilitating its ability to focus on long-term issues. The specific issues each committee will need to address as it moves through the year may vary, but the agenda should encompass both the immediate and the long-term work of the committee and the board.

Kevin Hoolehan, managing director of the Indiana State Foundation, and Larry Boulet, a member of the Indiana State Foundation board and partner at PricewaterhouseCoopers, effectively lay out new expectations for audit committees, while calling for a progressive agenda for the committee over the course of the year.

xi

How and when foundation board leaders should be called upon to help advocate on behalf of their host institutions in support for public higher education is the subject of the chapter by Carol Harter, president of the University of Nevada, Las Vegas, and John Gallagher, UNLV's vice president for advancement. The authors capably present both the risks and the rewards associated with involving foundation directors in the public-policy arena. This is a fine balancing act that requires significant planning and coordination between the institution and the foundation, and Harter and Gallagher offer some important lessons on how to create effective advocacy efforts.

As foundations and public institutions continue to seek new sources of funding, more of them are breaking new ground in establishing business ventures and alliances. Jerry Fischer, president of the University of Minnesota Foundation, offers some useful insights based on his own foundation's experiences about launching and sustaining entrepreneurial ventures that offer real potential — and real risks, as well.

Several useful appendices are included in this volume: Of special note are the new illustrative memorandum of understanding between a foundation and a host institution or system (developed jointly by AGB and the Council for Advancement and Support of Education) and a sample gift-acceptance policy. AGB's director of foundation programs, Doreen Knapp Riley, was instrumental in developing these important documents. I am grateful, too, to AGB Senior Editor Deanna

LaValle High and Vice President for Publications Daniel J. Levin, who ushered the manuscript through the publishing process.

Increasingly, the future of public higher education will rest with the men and women who serve on foundation boards. These dedicated volunteers commit their passion, generosity, and expertise in support of higher education. In many ways, the twin dreams of access and affordability — providing an opportunity for all to achieve their fullest potential — lie in the hands of these volunteers. Publication of *Margin of Excellence* continues AGB's commitment to the work of foundations and the special group of volunteers who serve on their boards. It is intended to facilitate their work and to acknowledge the importance of their contribution.

Public higher education — and the country as a whole — owe these volunteers an enormous debt of gratitude. With this in mind, we dedicate *Margin of Excellence* to these special individuals — the nearly 45,000 men and women who volunteer to serve as foundation directors.

RICHARD D. LEGON
Executive Vice President
Association of Governing Boards
of Universities and Colleges
Washington, D.C.

Margin of Excellence
THE NEW WORK OF HIGHER EDUCATION FOUNDATIONS

THE SHIFTING
LANDSCAPE:
*Challenges and
Opportunities*

The New Work
of Higher Education Foundations

Richard D. Legon

T he future ain't what it used to be!" So observed the 20th century philosopher Yogi Berra, with his usual prescience concerning societal forces. His assessment could be accurately applied to the more than 1,500 foundations that support public colleges and universities and higher education's important contributions to society. Yogi might be an effective herald for the changing landscape — already dramatically changed, some credibly argue — and the new realities facing these foundations and institutions.

A cursory history of foundations that serve public higher education illustrates the changed environment: The earliest foundations, dating to the late 1800s, were established to facilitate land acquisition and, eventually, to accept private gifts on behalf of public institutions. These organizations grew in number dramatically as higher education flourished in the late 1900s, especially as private support became an important, creative element in the expansion of land-grant and state institutions. New foundations sprung up as community colleges recognized the opportunities associated with a separately incorporated foundation.

The original relationship of institution and foundation was premised on a strong state commitment to support public higher education for its citizens. This social compact served the mutual needs of economic growth and personal opportunity. State leaders recognized public higher education as a top priority, and foundations affiliated with state institutions advocated with alumni and friends in support of special initiatives that would enhance an institution's ability to meet the state's interests. This mutual understanding had its ups and downs over the years as financial realities and pressing needs moved the bar graph of state resources in varying directions. Commitment to higher education as a public good was not in debate. That was then!

Across the states today, the reality is significantly different for public higher education. What society expects from colleges and universities no longer is clear. This chapter attempts to show how some of the financial, social, and political forces confronting public institutions are affecting the new work of higher education foundations and their volunteers.

The Changing Landscape

Public colleges and universities today enroll roughly three-quarters of all undergraduate students and nearly two-thirds of all graduate students. As elected leaders attempt to balance state budgets and come to grips with declining discretionary funds, the new financial realities facing public higher education have become clear. To address state trends, many institutions and systems are increasing tuition and cutting expenses. Other colleges and universities are advocating alternate financing arrangements with state leaders. The cuts — and the limitations of tuition increases to make up significant portions of budget shortfalls — are having significant effects on issues of access and global competitiveness, making it more difficult for public higher education to achieve its mandate.

With economic pressures forcing tough decisions and painful cuts, some important questions must be answered: Does the public truly understand the value a strong public higher education system brings to society as a whole and to individual students? How has financial support of public higher education changed? What does this shift mean for the foundations affiliated with state colleges and universities, and does the changed pattern of funding of higher education in recent years reflect a declining public commitment to the idea of the public university as a public good?

In recent years, we have witnessed shifts in public attitudes and policies that suggest that higher education is a private benefit to students, and therefore students and their families should bear a greater percentage of the cost. While it is undoubtedly true that students should shoulder a good deal of the costs of their education, we must not lose sight of the public benefits associated with higher education and the goal of making postsecondary education available to all.

Prevailing political will has focused the debate on the demand for greater institutional accountability. This focus and concomitant state-funding policy trends are likely to be with us for the foreseeable future, as positive economic news coming from many states is not likely to restore a pattern of more expansive funding for public colleges and universities. The debate also encompasses discussions of the economic development mission of public higher education within the states, and policymakers are reluctant to make the difficult decisions necessary to provide additional revenues through tax adjustments. Yet additional resources will be needed to meet growing enrollments and sustain expectations for quality. The ability of public colleges and universities to demonstrate their contributions to a state's strategic agenda and economy will become even more critical. Foundations and their boards will need to become involved in the debate on the public purpose of public higher education.

Foundation boards must recognize, however, that their host institution's governing board bears ultimate authority for establishing institutional priorities and policies. Broadened foundation board responsibility should not be confused with a greater role in institutional governance. Yet college presidents are looking more and more to their foundation boards to become involved in such areas as advancement, advocacy with public policymakers, marketing, and, in some instances, academic program review. Presidents walk a tightrope as they draw on the talents and influence of foundation board members while ensuring that the foundation board does not usurp the authority of the governing board.

In short, the landscape has altered for public higher education, and foundation board executives and directors should be aware of the implications of these changes on their own responsibilities.

New Priorities and Expectations

In light of changing expectations, foundations and their boards should revisit several past assumptions about their responsibilities. While not applicable to all institutions that have affiliated foundations, a new paradigm may well be in order for foundation priorities: Funding the institution's operations, public-policy advocacy, board-to-board collaboration, and joint planning initiatives are among the new or expanded priorities for foundation boards.

The critical quartet involved in executing these priorities includes the institution or system chief executive, the foundation chief executive, and the chairs of the governing board and the board of the foundation. These individuals should put their collective heads together to ensure that the institution and foundation operate synchronously and with a mutual understanding of expectations and responsibilities. With the stakes so high, institution and foundation leaders should work to ensure positive working relationships between the foundation and institution. The illustrative memorandum of understanding (Appendix C) suggests best practices for today's institution-foundation relationship.

Although it once sufficed for foundations to provide for the special opportunities — the margin of excellence — that allowed each institution to achieve its own unique attributes, this singular focus no longer is adequate to meet an institution's needs. Among the new expectations and challenges facing foundations are the following:

1. **Increased pressure to attract support for the institution's operating fund.** Coupled with the current political debate about who should fund public higher education is the economic reality in many states of a traditional tax base ill-suited to support the state's competing funding needs. Today's expanded institutional needs in an economy inadequately positioned to meet critical costs makes consideration of a new approach a necessity, not a luxury.

   The reality is (or likely will be soon) that foundations will be looked upon to help provide a growing portion of institutional operating funds. Because most funds raised and managed by foundations and institutions are restricted — they generally are earmarked for student scholarships, faculty support, capital projects, and research initiatives — this additional priority will require a new message aimed at conveying the current needs and overall value of public higher education. Some foundations will resist this level of involvement (as might some governing boards that will not welcome increased foundation involvement in institutional operations), but the realities of the altered landscape may well require this new role for foundations.

   As a consequence of the generous contributions of many endowments to their institutions in the 1990s, state officials and others have heightened expectations of what foundations reasonably can provide. Yet enhancements to physical plants, salaries, and scholarship aid enabled by endowment spending have added to the fixed costs of institutions. As a result, public colleges and universities and their foundation boards now find themselves in a double bind: On the one hand, declining support from state legislatures increases the pressure on foundations for institutional budget relief. At the same time, many endowments have not performed at levels that can sustain established spending expectations. Foundation boards, working through their investment and finance committees, must address this challenge in collaboration with leaders of the host institution.

   Similarly, foundation and institution leaders must not allow legislators to expect comprehensive campaigns, with their large financial goals, to substitute for their own continuing responsibility for public funding. Educating legislators about the distinction between the priorities of a campaign and the ongoing needs for operating support is essential work for foundation and institutional leaders.

6

2. **A new generation of donors.** While the opportunity exists for foundations to grow their assets significantly in the near term, much of the anticipated future growth of foundation assets will be the result of gifts from a new generation of donors. Although these young philanthropists already have shown a generous level of commitment, their interests often run counter to the growing pressure to raise operating support. Unlike more traditional philanthropists, many of the new donors prefer to actively oversee their gift dollars.

   How to balance the needs of the institution with the interests of this new generation of donors provides both an opportunity and a challenge for foundation leaders.

3. **Higher levels of collaboration.** In this lengthy period of uncertainty in public higher education funding, and with growing demands for increased accountability, foundations should seek opportunities to work collaboratively with their host institutions to advocate on behalf of the institution's funding needs. Developing a consistent message will require coordination between governing and foundation board leaders who can influence state policymakers.

   Recognizing the expanding responsibilities of foundations to advocate for and attract financial support, governing boards should welcome these colleagues as a source of advice and counsel in setting institutional priorities and strategies. Collaborative planning processes and retreats can help broaden foundation director awareness of academic program priorities, for example, while ensuring that the foundation board does not overstep its authority by reaching into governing board decision-making prerogatives and responsibilities. Collaborative planning opportunities also demonstrate the value of the foundation board as a source of future governing board members — and indeed the values of including a limited number of governing board members on the board of the foundation.

4. **Demands for greater financial transparency.** Scandals in the boardrooms of publicly traded corporations have resulted in demands for greater accountability and transparency, not only from corporations but from nonprofits of all kinds. Passage of the Sarbanes-Oxley Act of 2002, while aimed at the corporate sector, has had a significant effect on how nonprofit boards fulfill their responsibilities. Although some ardent supporters of Sarbanes-Oxley (including governing and foundation board members who also may be members of corporate boards) have suggested nonprofit boards should move aggressively to adopt portions of the law, foundation boards should review their

existing governance policies before codifying any new policies.

Sarbanes-Oxley is a healthy reminder to follow state laws and Internal Revenue Service regulations. Coupled with a review of the foundation's bylaws and conflict-of-interest policy, such a review can go a long way in assuring constituent groups that the organization is well governed. Nevertheless, legislative proposals in several states and the potential for federal action to mandate new nonprofit governance regulations bear watching.

In addition, new accounting guidelines — such as GASB Statement No. 39, which requires institutions regulated by the standards of the Government Accounting Standards Board to represent the foundation's financial activities as part of the institution's financial statement — pose additional challenges for many foundations and institutions.

Financial transparency is the new operational standard of increased accountability, and the realities of the creative, new funding strategies required to sustain the quality of public colleges and universities will continue to test that standard. In a certain sense, new financial reporting requirements serve to emphasize the increasing financial dependence of institutions on foundations. Again, the appearance of significant foundation assets should not be misinterpreted by legislators as an excuse to reduce state financial support, given the restricted nature of significant portions of foundation assets.

5. **Support for "bricks and mortar" initiatives.** Many foundations today are active in the acquisition and management of real estate holdings on behalf of their host institution. They also take on debt management through bond issuance on behalf of the institution's capital needs — often a politically complex and time-consuming undertaking. Through these kinds of initiatives, foundations seek to provide for the "bricks and mortar" needs of their institutions — further evidence that foundations are filling the void left by states that once routinely supported significant portions of these essential needs.

6. **Funding the costs of fund-raising.** Finally, as foundation boards are asked to lead and oversee aggressive fund-raising efforts on behalf of their host institution, the foundation must, if its resources allow, recognize its responsibility to absorb the costs of development efforts and those related to comprehensive campaigns. Public or institutional funding of these expanded fund-raising efforts is highly unlikely; the cost of a significant and permanent fund-raising infrastructure requires foundation support. Formulas for funding such costs vary, based upon the culture and history of the institution's fund-raising activities and the structure of the foundation. Nonetheless, support of

fund-raising costs is a vital part of the changing expectations of foundations.

The new landscape calls for a partnership dependent on coordinated, effective advocacy and expanded philanthropy. If public funding is not adequately restored as state budgets grow, it is only a matter of time before foundations are asked to assume even greater funding responsibility for the multiple operating needs of their host institutions. The reaction of current and prospective donors to this proposition is not at all certain.

Profile of the Future Board

How might this expanded set of responsibilities and expectations affect the profile of foundation boards? What characteristics should foundations add to the mix when seeking future directors? What challenges will foundations face in recruiting outstanding individuals to serve in light of increased pressure for new standards of fiduciary oversight? Do we risk limiting the pool of volunteers needed for foundation boards?

Certainly, boards need a range of expertise, the capacity to provide financial support, and the means to leverage personal influence with others of means. Other strengths are needed, too. Foundation boards should include people who understand how to make difficult decisions. Individuals with management experience who have faced the challenges associated with making tough choices generally are a good fit.

Those with financial management expertise (beyond investments) also add value, as do those who are politically astute and understand how public-policy decisions are made in state legislatures. Some foundation directors will need to be comfortable advocating with state leaders on behalf of institutional needs — the caveat being, of course, that neither individual foundation directors nor governing board members should advocate with policymakers unless they are conveying a consistent message as part of a coordinated strategy.

For foundations that serve multicampus systems with a systemwide governance structure (that is, individual campuses do not have their own governing boards), some directors will need to show an interest in the academic policy issues that normally confront governing bodies. Presidents of system-related campuses increasingly will reach out to foundation boards as something akin to a campus advisory board to test ideas and to participate in institutional planning. The changing landscape is likely to foster more personal and collaborative relationships among campus, system, and foundation executives, with a special focus on the strategic needs of the institution.

9

Impact on Institution and Foundation Relations

The president or chancellor of an institution must assume a central role in balancing the relationship between an institution's governing and foundation boards. The institution chief executive must develop a relationship based on mutual respect and premised on the best interests of the institution. While a foundation board should clearly understand that its focus must be on the essential priorities and needs of the institution, an institution's governing board should explore ways to demonstrate that it appreciates the value added by its affiliated foundation. The greater the presidential support and leadership in facilitating a mutual understanding and respect, the more foundations are likely to be supportive of institutional leadership.

10

In exploring a more active relationship, an initial order of business is for the institution and foundation chief executives to establish rapport with the respective chairs of the governing and foundation boards. If these relationships can be cultivated, the opportunity for a healthy, collaborative effort will be strengthened.

Institution presidents will be challenged to find ways to engage the two boards. Success will require a clear understanding of and respect for a foundation's legal status as an independent entity serving in the public trust. It also will require institution presidents to be perceived as fully committed to the foundation's responsibilities in fund-raising and advocacy. Presidents of public institutions must embrace their responsibility as the primary voice on behalf of the institution's fund-raising efforts. Foundation volunteers will be more inclined to be advocates when they see the institutional president actively engaged in fund-raising.

It may be tempting for foundation boards to weigh in on the president's performance, given that many foundations support portions of presidential compensation packages. It is appropriate for foundation board input to be sought for such periodic evaluations but only as it relates to the president's leadership of the fund-raising efforts or involvement in other areas of foundation responsibility. Foundation boards should not see their contribution to presidential compensation as providing them with extra influence in monitoring the president, as presidential selection and overseeing presidential leadership are governing board responsibilities.

Foundation boards will want to assess their own chief executives on a wide array of management skills, public-policy advocacy, and marketing prowess in addition to the traditional areas of fund-raising and investment management — if the board has decided these are priorities for the foundation chief executive.

Foundation chief executives always have had complex and challenging position descriptions, which often call on these leaders to be more diplomat than administrator or fund-raiser. Expectations and accompanying skill sets undoubtedly will grow even more complex in the future.

Working with institutional leaders, foundations also might consider ways to strengthen their relationships with faculty. Mutual understanding between faculty and the foundation can facilitate a healthier, more productive climate. Foundation boards might consider including faculty members or departmental deans in certain standing committee meetings. Faculty participation in the investment committee, for example, can help familiarize them with the complexities of the foundation's responsibilities. Presidents will benefit from their faculty's broader understanding of the foundation's work and the assets it oversees.

Changing priorities for foundations call for relationships that facilitate a clearer understanding of how their responsibilities and initiatives fit into the strategic plans of the college or university. Opportunities for joint planning between the foundation board and governing board — especially among their leadership — can facilitate a coordinated pursuit of institutional priorities. The relationship between institution and affiliated foundation should be based on a shared understanding of the current and long-term needs of the institution.

Shifting Sands

It's obvious that the "future ain't what it used to be" for foundations supporting public colleges and universities. As the states grapple with how to support public higher education, foundations will focus on helping these institutions serve an expanding student base that has diverse interests and needs. And as foundations attempt to attract operating funds for the institution and become more involved in institutional affairs, foundation board officers and senior staff will be confronted with growing demands, and in certain instances, legal challenges to the foundation's policies, especially in the area of privacy of donor records.

In addition to the courts, a number of state legislatures have been considering initiatives that could affect how foundations deal with this responsibility. While institutional leaders should be steadfast in support of foundation independence, recent court decisions suggest it is time for a fresh look at the question of donor privacy. Public pressure for greater transparency is likely to result in demands for unfettered access to expanded public information. Although states are addressing the questions with a range of responses, legislators and judges seem to be signaling support for more openness. In this unsettled environment, foundation and

11

institutional leaders will need to seek a balance, even as they seek to safeguard their financial support. They should have a strategy to determine what donor information should be released and they should be prepared to protect such competitive business information as prospect lists and sensitive information in a donor's record.

Rather than putting more onerous restrictions on foundations, however, state policymakers should be challenged to consider legislative initiatives that formally address the question of foundations as public agencies. Chapter 2 in this volume on foundation independence and the illustrative memorandum of understanding between an institution and foundation found in Appendix C provide some guidance and insight to help clarify the relationship between a foundation and its host institution.

12

Foundation boards will need to be flexible and nimble in responding to the shifting landscape. They will need to adjust their thinking and their priorities; they will have to be bold in accepting new challenges; and they will have to increase their tolerance for risk. There once was a time when public higher education recognized active foundations as "nice to have" because they enabled initiatives that made institutions special. Those simpler days are past. Today's and tomorrow's foundations are nothing less than a cornerstone of a vibrant public higher education agenda.

Foundation Independence and the Law

Thomas Arden Roha

F oundations that exclusively support a specific state university frequently are considered to be part of the university. If deemed part of the university, and thus part

of the state, the body of law that uniquely applies to states and state institutions will apply to the foundation as well. Among other things, this means the state's freedom of information act most likely will apply not only to the university but also to the foundation that serves it. Of particular importance to foundations is the privacy of donor information, as its release has the potential to create embarrassment for the foundation, the host university, and donors.

This chapter attempts to place independence in context for foundations that cannot achieve it — because of financial, legal, or political limitations — and to suggest actions foundations may take to protect themselves from the most troublesome application of state law, most significantly the state's freedom of information act. This chapter also assesses the state of the law on foundation independence as of July 2005.

What Independence Means for Foundations

There are a myriad of reasons why some foundations are not independent of the state colleges and universities they serve. Some lack the financial ability to exist independent of state aid. For others, the political atmosphere surrounding their university, donors, or the state itself makes pursuing independence impractical or impossible. Still others may believe they can better serve their state college or university by being dependent or interdependent. To clarify: Dependent foundations are wholly controlled by the college or university and rely on the institution for staffing, office space, and other support services. Many dependent foundations function as virtual subsidiaries of the institution they serve. By contrast, interdependent foundations are not fully controlled by the college or university, but they may take some benefits in the form of staff support, free rent, or other in-kind benefits.

Achieving independence is not necessarily a mandatory objective, and some state institutions may prefer a relationship with their related foundations that will not permit independence. Regardless, dependent and interdependent foundations can perform extraordinarily valuable services in behalf of the institution. They can own real estate, enter into contracts, have employees, hold and administer endowment and operating funds, and pursue and maintain relationships with donors, friends, and the community — all with the goal of enhancing the mission of the institution. These foundations can do so to the same extent as can purely independent foundations, but they must pursue their mission cognizant of the legal risks associated with interdependence and dependence.

Dependent and interdependent foundations, if separately incorporated, are independent to the extent their board of directors have fiduciary duties to the foundation, not to the college or university. This gives even the most dependent foundation room to argue that it is a different entity from the state institution and thus should not be subject to the laws that govern state entities. Moreover, most states thus far have yet to draw a bright line separating foundations that qualify as independent from those that are part of the state. Rather, the various laws reflect a frustrating lack of precision on issues of independence. But one person's frustration may be another's opportunity, and that lack of precision may be, for interdependent foundations, a handy tool they can use to proclaim their independence. Obviously, each unique state law ultimately will determine the meaning of independence for dependent and interdependent foundations.

Nonetheless, such foundations may be able to fend off requests under the state's freedom of information act for donor or other records or defend against allegations that some other statute that applies to the state also applies to the foundation. To do so, foundations should consider doing the following:

1. **Keep your lawyer involved.** Seek guidance from the foundation's lawyer on the extent to which the foundation is at risk under state law. This guidance should include not only the possible application of the state's freedom of information act but also its laws pertaining to open meetings, government contracts, competitive bidding, hiring and firing statutes, and so forth.

2. **Be aware of the foundation's degree of independence.** Review the "seven touchstones of independence" set forth in AGB Occasional Paper No. 39, and bring the foundation into compliance with as many as possible within the political and financial latitude available to the foundation. The touchstones

address the following questions: Does the foundation have an independent board of directors? Who pays for office space? Is the foundation served by university personnel? Does the foundation receive legal advice from the state attorney general? Is there suspicion that the foundation is engaging in improper conduct? Does the foundation routinely release all information about public funds? What does the agreement between the foundation and the university say?

3. **Release all information about public funds managed by the foundation.** If the foundation manages university funds or has received public funds for any purpose, it should separately account for those funds and release all information about how it uses or manages those funds. Just as a private donor to the foundation is entitled to know what the foundation is doing with his or her gift, taxpayers are entitled to know what the foundation is doing with public funds that are made available to the foundation.

4. **Be flexible on disclosure issues.** In our modern era of instant information, a hard-line no-disclosure rule will be greeted with suspicion and derision. Thus, unless foundation officials are highly confident they can defend against a freedom of information act request or any other challenge, a better course would be to adopt a flexible policy on public disclosure. This policy should provide for the release of as much information as possible, including the voluntary release of information on private funds absent a compelling reason in a specific situation not to do so. If the public ordinarily is provided with information about the foundation, chances are better that when an unusual circumstance suggests that a donor record should be withheld, the public may not be aroused. Moreover, a court charged with interpreting the state's freedom of information act could be influenced by the fact that the foundation's public-disclosure policy commits the foundation to releasing a broad spectrum of information. If the policy makes a reasonable case for withholding certain information, a court may feel less compelled to order the foundation to release sensitive information.

5. **Be prepared (the Boy Scouts have it right).** If the foundation receives a request for its records, there will be no time to call a committee meeting to formulate a response. Thus, anticipate that the foundation will receive a request for information and decide, in advance, how the foundation will respond under various scenarios. It may be useful to prepare a flowchart to guide the decision-making process foundation officials must go through in responding to such a request. The process should be approved by the

15

foundation's board, and the executive staff should be empowered to respond instantly to any request. Bear in mind, however, that if litigation ensues, the flowchart may well be subpoenaed. Foundation officials, therefore, should consider how media coverage will appear to the public.

6. **Lobby the legislature for protection.** It may be worthwhile to urge the legislature to enact a law protecting university-related foundations from certain applications of the freedom of information act and other laws. If donor records are a primary concern, then the foundation could align itself with the university to secure legislation that would protect such records held by both the foundation and the university. If broader protections are sought, the foundation could align itself with other university-related foundations in the state to forge a unified coalition.

A word of caution here: Many existing laws ostensibly designed to protect university-related foundations have ended up in a form that fails to effectively accomplish the protection. The legislative process is messy; good intentions can lead to poorly written or ineffective laws. If a foundation decides to pursue a lobbying effort, it must commit sufficient time, energy, and funds to ensure that it is effective.

In addition, most states have laws relating to lobbying, and foundation officials should familiarize themselves with their requirements before initiating a campaign. Moreover, Internal Revenue Service regulations stipulate that nonprofit organizations may not devote a substantial portion of their activities to lobbying. Foundation officials should be certain that any lobbying effort does not exceed those limitations.

The Emerging Legal Landscape

A foundation supporting a state university that accepts benefits from the state risks being deemed part of the state. The benefit can come in any form, but it most frequently comes in the form of provision of rent-free space in a state university building or the hiring of state employees to serve the foundation. Seemingly innocent benefits, such as a state university officer sitting on the foundation board or the attorney general providing legal advice, also lessen the degree of foundation independence.

Three recent court decisions are noteworthy:

• *Cape Publications, Inc. v. University of Louisville Foundation, Inc.*[1] In 2001,

---

[1] *Cape Publications, Inc. v. University of Louisville Foundation, Inc.,* Jefferson Circuit Court (September 18, 2003), Affirmed in Part, Reversed in Part and Remanded, *University of Louisville Foundation, Inc. v. Cape Publications, Inc.,* Kentucky Court of Appeals, No. 2002-CA-00150-MR (November 21, 2003).

a *Louisville Courier-Journal* journalist made a request to the University of Louisville Foundation pursuant to Kentucky's freedom of information act (known as the Open Records Act[2]), seeking the identities of donors and amounts they contributed toward establishment of the University of Louisville's McConnell Center. The foundation rejected the *Courier-Journal*'s request, claiming that the foundation was not a public agency and therefore not subject to the Open Records Act.

The trial court ruled otherwise and ordered the foundation to comply with the request for information. It also ruled that the act's personal privacy exemption would not protect the privacy of donor records. The foundation appealed to the Kentucky Court of Appeals.

The appeals court first affirmed the trial court's finding that the foundation was a public agency and then considered whether the Open Records Act's privacy exemption applied. The privacy exemption provision of the act was intended to prevent the release of such private information as tax returns, medical records, and the like — that is, information that individuals have a legitimate and reasonable expectation will not be released to the public. The appeals court ruled that whether the privacy exemption applied is a question of fact, and each gift therefore must be examined separately to determine whether the privacy exemption would apply. Since that question was treated as a question of law by the trial court, the case was remanded for factual findings on whether the privacy exemption applied.

Nonetheless, the court of appeals ruling that the University of Louisville Foundation is a public agency and subject to Kentucky's freedom of information act focused primarily on the following facts: (1) The foundation's initial incorporators were university trustees (even though the foundation was created at a time when the university was a private institution); (2) the foundation's board of 11 members included the university's president and four university trustees; (3) a university brochure said that the "foundation was founded to oversee funds donated to the university"; and (4) a substantial amount of the foundation's funding came from the state in the "Bucks for Brains" program, and the foundation could not legally receive those funds unless the foundation were, by law, an agent of the university. Moreover, the state funds managed by the foundation were not segregated from other funds held by the foundation.

In the appeals court's view, those facts compelled the conclusion that the University of Louisville Foundation received university benefits (that is, state benefits) and consequently is part of the university and part of the state. Thus,

---

[2] *KRS* 61.870 et seq.

Kentucky's freedom of information act applies to the foundation to the same extent it applies to the university or any other state agency.

Later, on remand, the trial court dealt with the appeals court's instructions to consider the factual question of whether the privacy exemption to the Open Records Act's privacy exemption applied. The trial court ruled that only those donors who had requested anonymity would be covered by the privacy exemption and, thus, the newspaper could have access to information about all other donors. Both sides appealed the trial court, ruling back to the appeals court — the newspaper wanting all records, even the records of those donors who specifically requested anonymity, and the Foundation seeking to have all donor records held exempt from disclosure under the privacy exemption. The Kentucky Court of Appeals, in an unpublished opinion, reversed the trial court and ruled, essentially, that all donor records should be exempt from disclosure.[3] The court stated that,

> . . . we conclude that the privacy interests of the donors to the Foundation outweigh the public interest in disclosure and hold that all of the records should be held exempt from disclosure. We believe that it does not matter whether a donor has specifically requested anonymity; the circuit court's logic in holding that a donor's request for anonymity somehow weighs in the analysis is flawed. We believe that unless the donor specifically waives the right to privacy, it should remain protected whether requested or not.[4]

The court's ruling that the foundation is subject to the state's open-records law means that the foundation's financial, personnel, and other records may be open to public inspection. The foundation's donor records are, however, exempt from disclosure under the privacy exemption.

- *Gannon et al. v. Board of Regents et al.*[5] The Iowa Supreme Court ruled in February 2005 that the Iowa State University Foundation is subject to Iowa's freedom of information act. The court reasoned that fund-raising is an essential function of Iowa State University, and the university could not avoid the application of the state's freedom of information act by outsourcing an essential function to an outside entity.

   In overturning a lower court ruling, the court ruled that the foundation performs a government function by virtue of its contract with the university;

18

---

[3]   *University of Louisville Foundation, Inc. v. Cape Publications, Inc. D/B/A The Courier Journal*, No. 2003-DA-002040-MR and No. 2003-CA-002049-MR (May 20, 2005) (Unpublished).

[4]   *Id.* at p. 6.

[5]   *Gannon v. Board of Regents*, Iowa Supreme Court, No. 131 / 03-1658 (February 4, 2005).

consequently, section 22.2(2) of the Iowa Freedom of Information Act mandates disclosure. The court further stated that "a government body may not outsource one or more of its functions to a private corporation and thereby secret its doings from the public." Iowa State University had a service agreement with the foundation and was involved in the creation of the foundation. The foundation was not supported by tax dollars, and only one university official was a voting member of the foundation's board. Moreover, the agreement between the foundation and the university portrayed the foundation as being an independent, private entity.

Despite the Iowa Supreme Court ruling, foundation officials have said the foundation will continue to withhold the names of donors who have asked for anonymity as well as personal donor information such as addresses, telephone numbers, and estate-planning documents. The foundation's ability to continue to withhold such information may be determined in subsequent litigation.

- *Affiliated Construction Trades Foundation v. University of West Virginia Board of Trustees et al.*[6] West Virginia University Foundation was erecting a building on private property owned by the foundation. The foundation intended to own the building, and a portion would be occupied by West Virginia University. An AFL-CIO affiliate sued the university and the foundation claiming that construction of the building was a joint venture of the foundation and the university and thus was "…a public project governed by the competitive bidding laws and prevailing wage laws of this state."[7]

  The trial court granted summary judgment for the foundation, ruling that it was not a public entity and not subject to the laws applicable to construction projects by public entities. The AFL-CIO affiliate appealed to the West Virginia Supreme Court. While the appeal was pending, construction of the building was completed. Although the case was technically moot, the West Virginia Supreme Court nonetheless agreed to consider the case, feeling compelled to explore the important public-policy issue of whether state funds were being expended consistent with state policy. (Although not noted by the West Virginia court, it is true that construction projects often are completed faster than court appeals; thus, courts might never be able to decide the important issues presented by the West Virginia University Foundation case if they simply dismissed all such appeals involving moot circumstances.)

  The West Virginia Supreme Court affirmed the lower court holding in

---

[6] *Affiliated Construction Trades Foundation, A Division of the West Virginia Building and Trades Council, AFL-CIO v. The University of West Virginia Board of Trustees, et al,* 210 W. Va. 456, 557 S.E.2d 863, 200 Lexis 194 (2001).

[7] 210 W. Va. 456, 461, 557 S.E.2d 863, 868. See also, West Virginia Code §§21-5A-1 to −11 (Repl. Vol. 1966 & Supp. 2001).

favor of the foundation, but the victory may be hollow. The reason is that the Supreme Court ruled that under certain circumstances, a construction project involving a West Virginia state university and its related foundation may be deemed a public improvement, thus triggering various statutes that apply to public construction projects, including competitive bidding and prevailing wage statutes. The court noted it was unable to determine from the facts in the record whether construction of the building by the West Virginia University Foundation should be deemed a public improvement. It also stated that the lower court should have undertaken a factual review sufficient to make that determination, but it refused to remand the case to the lower court for further factual findings.

Nonetheless, the West Virginia Supreme Court's ruling requires trial courts — in cases involving construction of a building by the foundation that will be used by the university — to make factual findings sufficient under standards articulated by the Supreme Court that will enable the trial court to determine which statutes that apply to state construction projects will apply in such cases. Although the West Virginia University Foundation case does not hold that such statutes necessarily apply to such construction projects, it is clear that facts suggesting a high level of involvement by the university in such a construction project would likely yield a conclusion that such statutes indeed apply.

What have these three recent cases added to the body of law? A safe conclusion is that they have not taken the law in a new direction but merely have affirmed existing trends. This certainly is true in the cases involving the University of Louisville Foundation and Iowa State University Foundation: A state university-related foundation risks being considered part of the state if it accepts benefits from the state. In some circumstances, however, minor state aid may not be problematic, as was the case involving the Iowa State University Foundation. In addition, the West Virginia University Foundation case serves as a useful reminder that statutes other than the freedom of information act that apply to state universities also may apply to university-related foundations.

Existing State Statutes

Some states have enacted statutes designed to protect university-related foundations. Some afford protection only from the state's freedom of information act; others are broader and offer protection from all statutes that apply to state entities.

For example, Minnesota has adopted a statute stipulating that donor information is private and not subject to public disclosure under the state's freedom of information act.[8] The Minnesota statute applies to the Minnesota Zoological Garden, the University of Minnesota, the Minnesota State Colleges and Universities, "and any related entity." Presumably, the language "any related entity" would include foundations that support the state universities in Minnesota.

Florida has adopted a statute that provides that a university-related foundation that meets certain criteria can use university facilities and personnel, and university officials may serve on its board of directors.[9] The statute requires that the foundation's books and records be audited by an independent certified public accountant, and the results of the audit must be provided to the state's auditor general and the state board of education. The statute specifically states that the identity of donors who desire to remain anonymous shall be protected.[10]

Louisiana has adopted a statute that, in essence, provides that a university-related foundation is a private entity and thus not subject to the state freedom of information act or other statutes that apply to state entities, so long as the foundation meets the following requirements:

- The majority of the voting members of the foundation's board of directors are not members or employees of a higher education management board (that is, the state university's board of trustees).

- The foundation is under the management and control of a board of directors elected by the contributing members or shareholders of the corporation.

- The foundation reimburses, either directly or through in-kind services, the cost of housing, personnel, and other support furnished to the foundation by the state university.

The requirement that the corporation have a board of directors elected by the "contributing members or shareholders" would disqualify many state university-related foundations since most of these entities do not have members. Rather, their boards of directors are self-perpetuating, meaning that the board is composed of individuals elected by the board itself, along with certain ex officio officials of the state university. One can only assume that the Louisiana statute is tailored specifically to protect that state's university-related foundations by adopting requirements that uniquely apply to these entities.

Georgia in 2005 amended its public-disclosure law to provide that records

[8] Minnesota Statutes, §13.792, Government Data Practices.

[9] Florida Statutes, §1004.28.

[10] *Id.* at §(5). The section also provides that, "[a]ll records of the organization other than the auditor's report, management letter, and any supplemental data requested by the State Board of Education, the University board of trustees, the Auditor General, and the Office of Program Analysis and Government Accountability shall be confidential and exempt from the provisions of section 119.07(1)."

maintained by public postsecondary institutions and their associated foundations that contain public information concerning donors or potential donors to such institutions or foundations shall not be subject to disclosure.[11] The Georgia law included a provision requiring disclosure of the name of the donor and the amount of donation if the donor or an entity in which he or she has a substantial ownership interest transacts business with the state institution.[12]

Colorado, too, amended[13] its public records law to exempt from disclosure records of an institutionally related foundation relating to donor identity, the amount of donor's gifts to the foundation and other information relating to the fund-raising activity of the foundation.[14] However, the new Colorado law specifically includes within the definition of a public record information of an institutionally related foundation relating to expenditures and requests for disbursements.[15]

A review of the various state statutes that offer protection to university-related foundations shows that none offers protection sufficiently crafted to ensure that such foundations will be treated as fully private entities. Even the otherwise well-intentioned and well-crafted Louisiana statute would fail to afford protection to a foundation with a self-perpetuating board of directors.

Some state statutes designed to protect the confidentiality of donor records cover only donors to the state university itself but afford no protection to donors to the related foundation. One would think that the public-policy reason justifying the confidentiality of information about donors to the state university would apply with equal force to information about donors to the university-related foundation.

No state statute, with the possible exception of Louisiana's or Colorado's, offers a university-related foundation protection from other state laws that apply to the state itself. The state legislature may simply have decided, as a matter of public policy, not to offer such protection. One must also assume, however, that any state legislature could craft a statute that (1) grants the public access to information in which it has a legitimate interest, (2) protects the confidentiality of donors and donor records, and (3) protects the foundation from unnecessary exposure to statutes governing the state itself, while encouraging university-related foundations to contribute to the growth and vitality of state universities. It would seem that such a statute has yet to be enacted.

---

[11] Georgia HB 340/AP signed into law as Act 359 signed by the Governor and effective May 9, 2005.

[12] *Id.*

[13] House Bill 05-1041 (signed into law and effective as of May 24, 2005).

[14] *Id.* at section 3.

[15] *Id.* at section 2.

Conclusion

Foundation officials must build relationships that will help the state university pursue and enhance its educational mission. Pursuing independence or legal protections for foundations that cannot achieve independence is not an end in itself. Such steps are merely part of various priorities that serve the goal of enhancing state-supported higher education. Each foundation must assess where independence fits on its priority list. It is not unreasonable for foundation officials to decide that maintaining independence is not a high priority. Interdependence between a foundation and a state university yields benefits that may outweigh the benefits of independence, especially in states where the legal environment is not hostile to dependent or interdependent university-related foundations.

23

We live in an era where state budgets are being squeezed. Public universities are being called upon to develop alternative revenue sources, and foundations are being asked to serve as the engines of growth for these universities. How a foundation can best accomplish this is vitally important.

Foundation Boards as Advocates

Carol C. Harter and John F. Gallagher

It would be difficult for college or university officials to overlook the troubling trend of declining state revenues for public higher education in the past several decades. Although actual public dollars spent on higher education have increased through the years, the percentages of average institutional budgets allocated by state legislatures have dropped significantly. Our own institution, the University of Nevada, Las Vegas, offers a good case in point: The state of Nevada supplied as much as 90 percent of the UNLV budget in the 1950s; today, funding is less than 35 percent, and UNLV considers itself fortunate to receive this amount. At many public institutions, including some of the most prestigious in the country, legislative appropriations now account for less than 20 percent of total university operating budgets.

Speculation abounds on the reasons for these declining percentages. Is it simply greater competition for state dollars among a growing number of critical yet expensive social programs? Is respect for higher education waning across the nation? Is the movement for greater accountability in government spending at the root? Naturally, these are compelling questions, but discovering the answers is perhaps less urgent than finding solutions to the budgetary woes the situation presents.

By necessity, most universities are attempting to find ways to grow other revenue sources; this is perhaps the most obvious and practical solution, and one that often yields impressive results. Yet higher education officials must consider another important and complementary strategy — cultivating advocacy on behalf of their institutions. In the interest of securing adequate levels of state appropriations, effective advocacy has become essential. Universities must pay close attention to developments in their state capitals and present legislators with persuasive information in support of their programs, research, and students. Such advocacy, however, should not be limited to discussions about how to obtain more state funding.

To appreciate this point, consider how important advocacy can be to the process of persuading public officials to accept alternate funding strategies. As higher education officials contemplate various entrepreneurial strategies aimed at enhancing institutional revenue streams, some activities may require a stretch of imagination on the part of legislators and governing board members. Some strategies inevitably will fall outside the traditional models for revenue generation and will require new ways of thinking about finance. Given the unconventional nature of some of these strategies, their endorsement by foundation and governing board members could make a critical difference in the decision-making processes of those with the authority to deny or accept unconventional funding ideas or mechanisms.

Although funding issues often are at the center of advocacy activity, there are a great many more subjects to be discussed by advocates and seemingly immeasurable benefits to be gained. Advocacy may be employed more aggressively for the greater institutional good on a number of fronts.

Advocacy Defined

The politically astute have used advocacy through the ages to advance causes in virtually all human endeavors. In contemporary higher education, individual institutions regularly coordinate the energy, commitment, and influence of their alumni and community leaders to influence legislators and other elected officials. Our focus here is limited to advocacy on the part of institutional volunteers — primarily foundation board members and program advisory board members — who many would consider the most natural and useful advocates for public institutions. We will also offer some commonsense definitions and, perhaps more important, discuss principles for establishing strong and productive advocacy and appropriate advocacy relationships.

In broad terms, advocacy by foundation board members may be considered any action taken in support of an institution. This may include discussing institutional goals with key political figures, facilitating public-private partnerships, representing the institution at a public meeting or event, or assisting in raising funds. In this context, it is reasonable to assert that advocacy is the *only* purpose of a foundation board, as these types of support are considered activities central to the responsibilities of a foundation board director. Simply put, advocacy takes many forms; for every goal an institution might develop, an advocate may be asked to explain and promote related issues and plans to various individuals or groups in government, private industry, the press, and other important constituencies.

Although institution and foundation officials have abundant expertise about the issues being considered by policymakers, the voice of the volunteer frequently carries greater influence. Political connections come in many forms, and the maxim "it's not *what* you know, but *who* you know" can serve the strategic needs of the institution well. Developing an effective, well-coordinated advocacy network is well worth the investment of time and effort.

Principles for Successful Advocacy Relationships

Any continuously productive use of advocacy requires institutions and their foundations to be systematic and consistent in their planning and use of volunteer advocates. Several principles of successful advocacy efforts offer insight to those who hope to employ advocacy strategies to advance institutional goals.

First, it is critical to identify the appropriate and best prepared individuals to represent the university as public advocates. Such persons already may be on the foundation or advisory board (and not simply by coincidence), or they may need to be recruited to join the cause. Although institutions ordinarily consider many qualities and attributes when identifying and recruiting board members, it may be desirable to recruit some as potential advocates on the basis of their relationship with specific individuals or groups. A prospect's special expertise — particularly if the issue is likely to be ongoing — is an important element in recruiting advocates, and it is essential that these individuals be carefully scrutinized with regard to potential conflicts of interest.

A central consideration in identifying an appropriate advocate is matching his or her passions with a given issue or project, especially when a great deal of effort is required. Genuine advocacy requires a passionate commitment; without an active interest, advocacy rings hollow. Zeal for a project, on the other hand, is communicated clearly and effortlessly.

A long-term project in which UNLV is engaged offers a good example. The institution seeks to redevelop the neighborhood and transform a major thoroughfare immediately to the east of the campus. Private landowners are involved, as are business owners, the county, the airport authority, the water district, the power and gas companies, neighborhood associations, and many others. Institutional officials naturally must work with representatives from all of these entities, as well as with other stakeholders in the university and the community. Leading this endeavor's advocacy efforts is a foundation director whose vision for the area has helped spark interest for the project in all quarters. This board member brings a contagious enthusiasm for the project to the campus

27

and the community and has helped create synergy between the university and the surrounding property owners. His passion for and dedication to the project illustrate just how important commitment and passion are to effective advocacy.

Although the task can be challenging, finding people who have the time and energy to devote to advocacy and the ability to influence outcomes is important. Influential community and business leaders typically are overcommitted, but they often find the time to support causes, projects, or issues *in which they have the greatest interest.* In fact, many of the best advocates are community members of some standing who are aware, engaged, and already busy. Institutions and foundations should not be deterred from recruiting such individuals.

For an advocate to be successful, he or she needs to be properly educated about the institution and its goals. This leads us to a second principle for building successful advocacy: It is extremely valuable for advocates to become well acquainted with the culture of the institution they are asked to represent. Academe is a highly specialized environment that, frankly, can require some explanation to the casual observer. Peer review, shared governance, and perhaps even academic freedom are complex notions that can seem unfathomable to those unfamiliar with university culture. Educating advocates about these and other important aspects of university life should be considered an investment in the individuals involved. The process has important implications for the time required of the president and the foundation chief executive, as well as with members of the senior management team. Effective advocacy cannot be accomplished without an investment from the highest levels of the institution.

At UNLV, several of our most effective advocates participated in a universitywide planning retreat, rolling up their sleeves to work with faculty, staff, and students to develop performance indicators for the institution's strategic goals. One participant — the chair of our foundation board — is also the CEO of a major gaming corporation (without a doubt, an overcommitted individual who nevertheless has found time to serve as an advocate). We appreciate our advocates' time and willingness to participate, and they have repeatedly expressed how useful these kinds of events are for them as they work to understand our university's culture, goals, and programs.

This type of exchange — of both knowledge and perspective — is crucial to successful advocacy. While we can help educate our advocates about the academy, one must remember that an effective advocacy relationship is a two-way street: Advocates should learn from us, and we, in turn, must respect and appropriately use the insight and abilities they offer.

Recognition of this important point leads us to the third major principle for cultivating effective advocacy: using and respecting advocates' business expertise. Members of the business community have keen insights into the local community and can help the institution and foundation navigate official bureaucracies efficiently, particularly in the areas of development and redevelopment.

Take again UNLV's neighborhood redevelopment efforts. Plans for this ambitious project may involve requests for zoning changes, infrastructure creation or modifications, or variations in traffic patterns in order to bring the redevelopment plan to fruition. All of these requests will require our advocates to interact with officials in various government agencies and with owners of surrounding land and businesses. To facilitate the university's efforts, private developers have served as valuable partners, achieving concrete and subtle results. Again, the people who serve in this capacity deserve to know that their views, time, and expertise are valued; there is no better way to achieve this than to put their finer qualities to demonstrably productive use.

29

Coordinating the Message

Developing and coordinating an effective advocacy initiative requires active oversight on the part of institution and foundation officials. The process is not automatic, and successful advocacy is seldom accidental. For example, if a foundation director is asked to speak to an elected official in favor of legislation favorable to the institution, the mechanics of the contact must be properly managed. The timing and arrangements of the visit or conversation must be carefully planned and organized, and the director fully briefed. All of the logistics must be coordinated in a way most likely to produce a positive outcome.

An important element of planning and managing the initiative is ensuring that the message being advocated is consistent with the objectives of the institution and the foundation. Coordination is essential; policymakers and community leaders will quickly dismiss the institution's case if they receive multiple messages.

Some institutions and foundations have established ad hoc committees or task forces within their governing bodies or foundation boards to oversee public-policy and advocacy goals. Whether such a body is appropriate for all situations depends on the culture and structure of the board. Nevertheless, a process should exist to ensure that advocacy messages are clear and consistent with institution and foundation goals.

The Political Context

With all of these constructive ideas for the selection, development, and coordination of advocates and support of their work, advocacy might seem to be a fairly cut-and-dried process. Not necessarily. The entire endeavor must be conducted with great sensitivity. Advocacy, after all, is a political function that naturally carries the usual risks and challenges associated with politics.

Analyzing the broad political environment and the more subtle contexts before beginning an advocacy effort is an essential first step. Depending on the circumstances, the process can be straightforward, or delicate, or somewhere in between — but nuances, perspectives, and personal relationships can affect how the process unfolds. All of these variables will affect an advocacy effort.

Perhaps the most critical relationship to consider is the one between the boards of the foundation and the institution or system. One board or the other may see itself serving as the lead advocate on every issue or on a particular matter. Unresolved, this can present significant challenges, especially if the various participants have strong personalities. Presidents and system heads, working with foundation and governing board leaders, need to assess the best approach. The chairs of the governing and foundation boards may be especially helpful in negotiating the respective roles. It is especially important that everyone involved considers the university a "partnership" in which mutual objectives are the consensus priority, rather than simply a collection of loose affiliations with different goals and strategies.

Working together, university and foundation leaders can foster appropriate advocacy relationships and effective communication between the respective boards and other key political bodies. The following strategies may prove helpful:

- Ensure that advocates and other spokespersons comprehend and can articulate consistent messages in behalf of the institution.

- Identify and discuss mutually agreed-upon positions on issues that serve as starting points for the language of advocacy.

- Encourage senior staff to form strong relationships with advocates and key political figures so that they can follow the decision-making processes.

- Prepare advocates by providing them with whatever materials and/or assistance they need to be effective, including comprehensive background information, possible responses to difficult questions, and logistical support.

- Keep the passions and interests of advocates directed toward university priorities.

- Recruit advocates and form solid relationships with key constituencies well before controversy or crisis situations erupt.

- Finally, the number of advocates *on any specific issue* should be limited to those who can be the most effective, based upon their expertise and connections with decision makers. Not every trustee, regent, or foundation director can be an effective advocate, and it can be counterproductive to have individuals who take on advocacy assignments independent of a coordinated effort. When establishing an advocacy team is worthwhile, it might be worth considering including volunteers from both the governing body and the foundation board.

Promoting, cultivating, and building advocacy relationships require time and attention. Many skilled higher education leaders have developed abilities that can help guide the advocacy process and engender its success. There are, after all, a great many gains to be made through such efforts. We often call our advocates "friends of the university" with good reason: The value of a friend cannot be overestimated.

31

The Entrepreneurial Foundation

Gerald B. Fischer

As foundations affiliated with public colleges and universities have grown in size, strength, and sophistication, they have experienced increasing demands — and opportunities — to "do good" for their host institutions in ways other than traditional fund-raising and asset management. Financial pressures on public higher education have increased in recent years as state government investment has not kept up with the needs of public colleges and universities. University leaders are requesting or even pushing foundations to consider higher risk strategies to achieve increasing returns on assets or to find new revenue sources to benefit their institution. A question heard frequently in recent years is "How can we leverage private support — tangible and intangible — most effectively?" These opportunities differ from the normal functions of foundations. Often, they are projects that the university itself cannot perform for legal reasons, that the university would not accomplish as effectively, or that the university would be uncomfortable pursuing on its own.

Opportunities to pursue "nontraditional" activities are increasingly a fact of life for institutionally related foundations regardless of their size or the type of public institution they support. Foundations are being asked to consider unusual investments or activities because their essential characteristics make them inviting collaborators: independent legal status, specialized expertise among board members, and good reputations for "getting things done well."

How can foundation boards choose wisely among options — indeed, decide whether or not to pursue proposed opportunities at all? Institutionally related foundations considering new entrepreneurial activities should examine several criteria before taking on — or passing up — any opportunity. Each foundation has its own set of strategic priorities, values, and culture, and what works for one organization may not fit another. While the differing historical, tax, and legal environments facing specific foundations could lead their executives and directors to different decisions, the criteria presented in this chapter may serve all as useful guideposts for directors and senior staff.

33

A Foundation's Mission

The purpose of most institutionally related foundations is to engage private resources to enhance the excellence of their sole beneficiary, a public institution of higher education.

Through their status as independent legal entities, foundations help assure donors and prospective donors that their gifts will not be commingled with public funds and thereby possibly diverted to a purpose other than what the donors desire. The private resources marshaled by the foundation include not only the financial support that donors provide, but also the wisdom and work provided by the board and other volunteers.

To carry out their missions, foundations pursue a range of core activities: recruitment of high-quality directors to serve on their boards and campaign committees; strategic and professional fund-raising; stewardship of donated assets through active investment management; and ensuring appropriate expenditures of gift proceeds. To support these general functions, foundations also provide the normal infrastructure — accounting, information technology, donor prospect research, planned giving services, prospect coordination, communications, event planning, and so forth.

Usually, foundation performance is measured by the number and size of new gift commitments made during a fiscal year, the total asset base, the endowment size, the total investment return, monies disbursed to the host institution, and other indicators of effectiveness such as the cost to raise a dollar. As independent legal and financial entities, however, foundations can go beyond such "plain vanilla" functions as professional fund-raising and funds management. Foundations can move more quickly, flexibly, and with less bureaucracy than most public agencies. They increasingly are a source of financial strength and power. Their directors, in particular, can be of enormous support to the foundation chief executive in articulating to key stakeholders the rationale either for undertaking a new activity or for not doing so.

Nontraditional Entrepreneurism

Several types of nontraditional or entrepreneurial activities recently have occupied the time of foundation executives and boards. The Internal Revenue Service classifies several of these activities as "unrelated business," which may make any income they produce subject to income-tax. Some examples:

- Purchasing, developing, and/or managing real estate for university expansion, student housing, retirement communities, or solely to increase foundation revenue with no direct connection to a university purpose.

- Owning facilities on university property.

- Investing in promising university research.

- Holding licensing agreements and other forms of intellectual property.

- Borrowing or guaranteeing the debt issues of third parties.

- Leasing or owning aircraft for university or foundation use.

- Leasing or owning research equipment for use by university faculty or students.

- Facilitating or investing directly in industry-university collaborations.

- Investing endowment assets in the university's technology-transfer activities.

- Expending unrestricted gift proceeds as grants for strategic projects or for which no other natural funding source exists.

- Investing endowment assets in "alternative" investments.

- Holding, managing, or operating business enterprises (often received as gifts).

- Selling or swapping donor lists.

- Facilitating or brokering corporate sponsorships or exclusivity contracts.

- Licensing or selling the foundation's own technology, Web site contents, or other intellectual property.

- Implementing an incentive-based, supplemental compensation plan for the professional development staff.

All items on this list have been considered or undertaken by major institutionally related foundations in recent years. The University of Minnesota Foundation (UMF) has considered virtually all the ideas on this list. After thorough analysis and consultation with our directors and outside advisers, we implemented only some of the proposals.

Assessing New Activities

Several questions and criteria are pertinent in considering any foundation activity, either existing or prospective. Each foundation has its own set of strategic priorities, values, and culture, and what works for one organization may not fit another.

The criteria that follow reflect the priorities, values, and specific circumstances of the University of Minnesota Foundation. While the differing historical, tax, and legal environments facing other foundations could lead their executives and directors to make different decisions, the following criteria may serve as useful guideposts in deciding whether to undertake innovative, entrepreneurial, or nontraditional activities: (1) mission fit; (2) sound financial management; (3) capacity of board; staff and other resources; (4) diversion of management talent; and (5) perception of key constituencies.

Mission Fit. Does the proposed activity have high integrity with the mission of advancing the excellence of the college or university? Does the activity represent a probable or likely diversion or drift from the core mission? There will be many tempting opportunities to do good work for the college community, for the students, for the faculty. But foundation leaders must constantly ask this question: Does the inviting idea fit with what the foundation was created to do?

Our foundation would resist activities that promise to build the foundation without a close or direct connection to advancing the university. For example, it would be difficult for us to accept owning, managing, and operating a company donated by an alumnus whose sole purpose would be to earn higher revenue for the foundation. On the other hand, we created a company as a for-profit subsidiary of the foundation to own and operate supercomputers that would be available to faculty and students as well as to industrial clients. The foundation board provided most of the board members for the subsidiary. And, after several years of operation during which we obtained the foremost computing power in the world and made it available to the university community on favorable terms, we sold the corporation to a third party and earned a handsome capital gain.

This nontraditional, entrepreneurial activity used the special strengths of the foundation to advance the university. Therefore, it was considered an excellent fit with our mission.

Though there were many challenges in operating the company and communicating the rationale for the foundation's involvement to donors, legislators, and others, starting the subsidiary proved to be a winning strategy. Providing convenient access to state-of-the-art supercomputing on attractive economic terms was an important factor in the university's ability to recruit and retain outstanding faculty from the early 1980s to the mid-1990s, not to mention the profound research and many discoveries it also facilitated.

Sound Financial Analysis. The foundation board or appropriate board committee (the finance or executive committee, for example) should ensure that staff conducts thorough homework on the financial reality of any nontraditional opportunity. Most foundations have limited resources. Unrestricted funds are especially scarce. No foundation can afford to undertake activities that represent an ongoing or significant potential drain on its resources or that threaten its core functions. A common warning many development professionals cite that I heartily endorse: "Don't accept gifts that eat."

37

Before accepting any gift of real estate or an operating company, for example, our staff performs due diligence, going through a checklist of potential liabilities and risks.

It also is important to understand whether the proposed activity is consistent with the nonprofit purposes of the foundation or whether it involves special tax treatment, such as the unrelated business income-tax (UBIT). If so, the activity may involve establishing a for-profit subsidiary of the foundation as well as separate, specialized accounting treatment. A proposed activity involving UBIT may be completely worthy and acceptable, but everyone involved must understand the implications in advance. The Association of Governing Boards, the National Association of College and University Business Officers, and other national associations have resources available to suggest best practices.

Various funding sources may be possible for nontraditional activities. The proposed activity may involve using the foundation's reserves, a specific donor fund, or the investments supporting the foundation's endowment. The financial analysis should include relevant return thresholds and other tests appropriate to the funding source. For example, using endowment assets to own an equity position in a new company being formed around a research discovery from a professor's laboratory brings with it the compelling argument of achieving two goals at once — potential investment return and supporting faculty in technology transfer.

In such cases, however inviting, it is crucial that the investment tests be the same as for all other investments in the endowment. Do the projected risks and returns fit the profile for the rest of the portfolio? This test is important to ensure the fiduciary responsibility of the board is not being compromised. Any use of endowment assets should stand the test of a review by the foundation's investment committee.

Likewise, if the proposed activity involves tapping the reserves or unrestricted funds of the foundation, the financial analysis must include an assessment of what other opportunities exist for using these scarce resources. Prioritizing all scarce resources — financial, personnel, and technology — is an essential discipline of any well-functioning business.

A good financial analysis must include a thorough look at all potential financial risks or exposures. Many such risks can be indemnified or may be deemed acceptable without the acquisition of insurance. My main point is that all decision makers must be aware of the risks through a realistic assessment before the decision is made.

As foundations have grown in size and sophistication, the option of entering into borrowing arrangements has emerged as an intriguing mechanism to leverage assets more effectively — either to accelerate capital projects or to realize more financial power from the endowments beyond the typical annual spending policy of 4 percent to 5 percent. It becomes particularly inviting to consider using this method to accomplish high-priority strategic projects when interest rates are at historically low levels. If the project qualifies, the use of tax-exempt financing may be advantageous and could be obtained either by private placement or in the public markets.

The public-market option may entail meetings with the debt-rating agencies, preparation of prospectus descriptions of the project's financial viability, and various covenants. The debt-rating agencies may view foundation assets and liabilities as an extension of the host university financials. In that context, the borrowing activity of the foundation may affect the university's debt rating or borrowing capacity.

Within the last several years, the University of Minnesota Foundation found it advantageous to guarantee a tax-exempt, revenue bond offering. We used this strategy to fund the construction of a new office building and alumni/welcoming center on the flagship campus of the university. UMF, the University of Minnesota Alumni Association, and the Minnesota Medical Foundation created a jointly owned, private nonprofit corporation. UMF had the financial strength to guarantee the performance of the affiliated corporation that was formed to build the $46 million, 235,000 square-foot construction project and operate it.

The university and three "owner" organizations agreed to lease the entire office space for at least ten years. The resultant lease payments would more than service the $40 million debt offering. Private gifts were raised to build and furnish the public reception and meeting spaces in the alumni/welcoming center as well as an adjacent park. The guarantee, for which UMF is paid a fee, is treated as an off-balance-sheet liability of the foundation. Two of the national debt-rating agencies assigned a debt rating to the guarantee, which extended to the debt offering.

We regard this mechanism as highly appropriate because it furthered the mission of the university as well as the missions of the three organizations. It made good sense financially, permitting the project to be funded at an attractive cost of capital, supported entirely by the financial characteristics of the project itself. There is a low likelihood of any claims being made on the foundation or any of the other owner organizations, and the financial model provides for the buildup of reserves to cover long-term contingencies and replacement of major operating systems.

A word to the wise on conducting a thorough financial analysis: Respect and impose the discipline of an objective assessment of the financial risks and opportunities involved in any proposal. Often, successful foundations come to be regarded as the university's "inside bank." Those who view foundations this way see them as an unending source of operating and capital resources to be called upon to solve virtually any problem or need that may arise at the host university.

There will never be a shortage of worthy ideas to advance or rescue outstanding programs within the academy. To respond to appeals for support, the foundation must have well-grounded information on each opportunity to help determine the best decisions or to rank multiple proposals on their financial merit.

What does a foundation board chair do with the financial analysis? If the project is not financially viable, and if acceptable terms cannot be achieved through negotiation, then it should be rejected. This may be extremely difficult to do, especially if a beloved university president or a committed and active volunteer or donor has suggested the project. Nevertheless, the long-term health of the foundation and to the discipline of well-informed and sensible decision making must be the bases for the final judgment.

The final set of criteria relate more to the "how-to-implement" aspects of the activity rather than to the "what" of the decision, which is addressed by the first two criteria. I have observed that a great strategy poorly implemented will fail, while a flawed strategy that is well implemented will be widely regarded as a success. So, the issues surrounding a successful implementation often are as important as the criteria applied to deciding whether the project is a good one in the first place.

Capacity of Staff and Other Resources. Foundation leaders should carefully consider whether it makes sense to take on a new activity without gauging the staff's expertise or competence or without adding additional staff. In many

39

cases, it may be necessary and appropriate to outsource some functions. Outside expertise may be useful, for example, in developing, building, and managing real estate projects or an investment portfolio involving venture or intellectual capital.

It may be appropriate for the board to form a task force or ad hoc committee, including directors with professional expertise in the proposed initiative. Such a group could provide great service in analyzing the opportunity, developing successful implementation strategies, and overseeing at least the initial stages of the strategy's execution. The degree of involvement by the board in analysis and initial implementation would most likely be a function of the degree of risk or potential risk in the proposed activity.

As UMF pursued the new alumni/welcoming center and office building, we hired an owner's representative to track the design, development, construction, and launching phases of the project. No such expertise existed within the staff. Though we drew heavily on the expertise of volunteer leaders for overall project management, financial analysis, and fund-raising, we used outside resources for special functions throughout the project.

Another important task is to assess the potential effect of a new project on the foundation's management, financial control, and information systems. Does sufficient capacity exist to absorb the new initiative? Is new software needed? Can existing systems be adapted to the new activity easily, or will this be difficult? Are special accounting, tax, or legal treatments needed?

Diversion of Management Talent. Adding any new activity inevitably will involve additional work and attention from the chief executive, staff financial officers, and other senior managers. The key issue is the extent to which the new activity may divert the senior staff and/or board attention from the core functions of the foundation.

UMF has resisted some potentially attractive opportunities because we were concerned that these could disrupt the organization's focus on a capital campaign. A case in point involved a student housing project. An outside developer proposed to buy property near the campus, build a unit with 500 beds, work with the city government to obtain all necessary permits, and then turn the project over either to the university or to the foundation at a "bargain price." The university had identified as a major priority the expansion of on-campus or near-campus student housing. The financial analysis indicated a marginal deal at the terms presented.

The deal-breaker, however, was our concern regarding the management time required to negotiate an attractive financial arrangement and then to determine how best to manage the property for the long run with minimal operating risk.

To minimize the risk of a diversion from higher priorities, the foundation would have had to hire an expert to track the project, consult with university housing staff, and then operate the facility. The need to hire additional staff expertise adversely affected the already marginal financial analysis, but a major obstacle for us was the potentially large claim on our leadership resources to ensure a successful endeavor. In many ways, time is our most precious commodity. How leaders choose to commit that time communicates the top priorities to an entire organization.

Perceptions of Key Constituencies. A foundation's reputation is built over many years with donors, alumni, and friends; business, community, and government leaders; and with the university president, regents, deans, chancellors, and other administrative and faculty leaders — not to mention the foundation's own board and staff. Maintaining the foundation's "trust compact" with key stakeholders must be a top priority. Communication plans should be developed to clarify the rationale, motives, and attractive features of each nontraditional activity. Also, a clear statement of how the activity fits with the mission of the foundation is essential.

How does this new enterprise advance the excellence of the foundation's sole beneficiary — the university? If it is difficult to articulate how the proposed activity fits the university's mission, the difficulty may signal danger. If too many constituents perceive that "the leopard is changing its spots," then the trusting environment you have enjoyed will change dramatically as the foundation becomes more defensive in articulating its reason for being.

A clear, effective, and compelling communications plan should include face-to-face meetings with the influence leaders within the key constituencies. Maintaining the trust requires openness in attitude and style. Aside from maintaining the confidentiality of all donor, prospect, and employee files, it is important to answer all questions about operations, whether from close associates, colleagues from other organizations, or the press. Answering questions candidly is an opportunity to build greater understanding and trust.

In thinking about a communications strategy, do not underestimate the importance of internal audiences, especially the university president and the governing board. It is crucially important that the beneficiary be comfortable and confident with the foundation. "No surprises" is a rule of good relationships and good management.

The Trust Compact

As institutionally related foundations continue to build large asset bases and demonstrate how engaging private support effectively can uplift the quality of their host universities, more opportunities to pursue nontraditional activities will present themselves. By applying various screens and criteria in assessing these opportunities, foundation leaders can increase the likelihood of successfully implementing new strategies and avoiding pitfalls. The "trust compact" of authority and confidence developed throughout any foundation's life is so valuable that no nontraditional activity a foundation undertakes should undermine its ability to perform its core business.

A SAMPLE ENTREPRENEURIAL ACTIVITY OF THE UNIVERSITY OF MINNESOTA FOUNDATION

Developing a Biotech Incubator Facility

One of the University of Minnesota's top priorities is to strengthen its technology-transfer capabilities. A recent study chaired by the dean of biological sciences and the director of the entrepreneurial studies program recommended the university build a biotech incubator facility on or near the campus. The study advocated a nonprofit structure and private fund-raising for the project, an approach that would be faster and more effective than any attempt to gain approval through the capital-planning process at the university. Also, private development likely would offer opportunities to involve industry partners in the planning and development. The university president agreed that this project was a high priority and asked that it quickly proceed.

UMF was asked to assume a leadership role, which included using its nonprofit status and working with potential corporate partners. In evaluating our potential participation, we applied the criteria discussed in previous pages:

- First, there was a good fit with our mission. A clear connection existed between the university's ability to attract and retain top faculty and graduate students and an environment that encourages the movement of ideas from the laboratory to the marketplace. We concluded that an incubator would help foster such an environment.

- Second, the financial analysis was compelling, whether the facility would be located on campus or nearby.

- Third, a recent expansion of our finance office provided a level of expertise that could provide day-to-day stewardship of our participation. Also, an excellent candidate was identified to be the project leader, and we engaged an "owner's

representative" for real estate development/ construction projects.

- Fourth, we were concerned that a long-run involvement would suggest too much of a hands-on role in an activity that could become a diversion from our primary role of leading fund-raising. Therefore, we agreed to facilitate the launch and indicated that our involvement timeline would be limited.

- Fifth, we believed our key constituencies would be supportive of our helping to create an asset to advance this dimension of the university's research mission.

In the end, we decided to play a facilitative rather than a controlling role. Initially, the project can take advantage of our nonprofit status until we find another acceptable nonprofit owner. The foundation may make a minority investment if that would help encourage other investors. We are using foundation counsel to guide the legal and tax aspects, and the foundation has provided start-up operating funds.

This project is still evolving. These things often take more time than expected, and opportunities are fluid. We may renovate a facility rather than build a new one, and because the available building offers more space than needed for the original scope, we may consider renovating more space. Interest is high among prospective collaborators. Meantime, research conferences are being planned to bring scientists and venture representatives together, and the potential for future gifts is clearly evident.

43

Margin of Excellence
THE NEW WORK OF HIGHER EDUCATION FOUNDATIONS

HERE AND NOW:
Standing Committees of the Foundation Board

The Committee on Directors

James L. Lanier, Jr. and E.B. Wilson

No foundation committee is more vital to overall and long-term board performance than the committee on directors. Foundation boards require that directors exercise diligent, energetic, and professional leadership as they act as stewards of the financial resources of the foundation and as the locus of philanthropic support for the host institution. The quality of this stewardship contributes significantly to the successful management of the foundation's financial resources and to the vigor of cultivation and solicitation of new sources of funding. Few conditions are more damaging to a foundation's vitality than the apathy of an inert board of directors.

The committee's principal responsibilities include assembling the right mix of director talent, educating and organizing that talent, assessing director and board performance, and motivating and rewarding directors.

Committee Charge

What is the core governance role of the committee on directors? Against what standards should the performance of the committee be measured? While mission ideas and concepts are more important than specific language, each foundation's committee on directors should write its own charge, with the following offered as a place to start:

The committee on directors is charged with determining the most effective composition of the board. It develops practices and recommends strategies and policies that attract, orient, educate, organize, motivate, and assess the performance of directors. Through its work, the committee provides the foundation board with the director resources that permit the board to exercise its responsibilities for foundation governance at the highest level of excellence.

The committee cannot effectively begin its work before it and the full board have a comprehensive understanding of the foundation's strategic direction. This requires that the committee, the board chair, and the foundation's chief executive officer enter into a continuing and comprehensive dialogue about the strategies the foundation will deploy to accomplish its strategic mission. From these understandings, the board develops the strategic direction of the foundation — a critical determinant of the foundation board's composition.

Committee Responsibilities

The responsibilities of the committee are a continuum of practices and policies that begins with an understanding of the board's present and future needs for talent and ends with finding ways to motivate and communicate with directors who have retired from the board.

1. **Define board composition.** The mission-central responsibility of designing the board's composition should begin with an analysis of the current board's attributes. This should include the following:

   - a baseline to record each individual's years of service as a director, gender, ethnicity, geographic location, and educational background;

   - occupational credentials, showing for-profit and nonprofit experience, specific professional expertise, and board or governance experiences;

   - an analysis of functional expertise and reputation;

   - a confidential assessment of personal giving capacity;

   - a confidential analysis of giving history; and

   - an analysis of each director's personal and professional spheres of influence.

2. **Project an "ideal" profile for the board's composition three years out.**

   The committee's goal is to build the best board possible, reflective of the aspirations of the institution and the mission of the foundation. Establishing a future model for the board will assist the committee when it begins to evaluate candidates for each new class of directors. This exercise should address the following questions and should be reviewed annually:

   - What will be the effect on the board if its composition remains the same?

   - Does the present board reflect the foundation institution's constituencies and donor base?

   - Is it appropriate to change the age composition of the board to represent a changing donor base?

- Is it appropriate to change the geographic profile or should the gender or ethnicity balance be changed?

- What kinds of technical or functional expertise will the board require (legal, fund management, real estate, trust, or audit)?

- How will new directors affect the "institutional memory" of the foundation and the institution?

- Does the institution's strategy suggest that a new capital or comprehensive campaign should be launched? As a result, will the foundation board require a higher level of fund-raising experience?

- Does the board have the right balance of affluence and influence — the capacity to give and the skills to persuade?

- Does the pipeline of future board leadership contain sufficient talent to ensure a continuation of the foundation's professional vitality?

- Will anticipated retirements from the board leave significant talent gaps?

Ideally, the committee should define the skills and attributes it desires in new members, and then seek the individuals who possess those characteristics. However, it is not unusual for some political systems, institutional charters, and foundation bylaws to help determine foundation board composition by requiring that specific constituencies be represented in perpetuity. Although these requirements reduce the flexibility of the board to determine its composition, they do not alter the direct linkage between board composition and the fulfillment of the foundation's mission. It is incumbent on the committee on directors to hold each member of the board — regardless of their route to directorship — accountable to the other directors, to the foundation, and to the institution. All members should go through the same orientation program, work on committees and task forces, and be fully engaged. They can, in these ways, augment the talent profile of the board and contribute to the fulfillment of the foundation's responsibilities.

3. **Write a statement of criteria.** This statement will reflect the broad-stroke understandings about the attributes the committee should be looking for in director candidates. It can serve as a screening tool for the committee when it begins to narrow a long list of possible candidates down to a prioritized short list. Assigning numerical weights to each criterion is a further refinement to assist in ranking candidates.

4. **Develop and manage a network of new-director candidates.** There are three steps here:

    Build and maintain a "watch list" of potential directors. In effect, the committee should be engaged in a continuous search; it should maintain an inventory of candidates from a variety of sources, including foundation board members, the chief executive officer, senior fund-raising professionals, college or university leaders, as well as donors and other alumni leaders.

    Cultivate and ask candidates. Each candidate on the watch list requires a careful strategy designed to assess his or her interest, develop or renew a connection to the institution and the foundation, and anticipate what it will take to persuade the candidate to serve. Often, the best candidates are busy and already involved with other worthy agencies or endeavors. Cultivate board members as one does a donor. It may take several years, but the rewards for the organization can be well worth the time, effort, and attention to detail.

    Make recommendations to the board. This is an opportunity for the committee to reinforce its mission with the full board. Biographical data for each candidate should be made available to each board member in advance of election. The committee chair should connect the candidate with the board-composition strategy by linking the candidate's background and experience to the criteria statement of forecasted talent needs.

5. **Develop and manage an orientation program for new directors.** Orientation for new directors begins when the board chair puts down the phone after the welcoming call. It should be executed in four phases.

    Provide a briefing package. Within a few days of appointment, the new director should receive briefing materials and a letter of welcome jointly signed by the board chair and the committee chair. It also is appropriate for the chief executive and the committee chair to welcome new directors with a phone call or note.

    Assign a mentor. Mentors should be sitting directors with sufficient years of service to know how the board works — its ambiguities and idiosyncrasies. Phone calls and other communications both before and after meetings will help new directors surmount the learning curve. Not to be forgotten is the need to train mentors. Prepare a short statement of responsibilities, and include a suggested calendar of contacts for mentors and new directors that covers at least the first year of service.

    Implement a formal orientation program. This should be a high-profile program attended by the board chair, the institution's president, the foundation's chief executive, and the new director's mentor. The following agenda accomplishes the full scope of orientation objectives:

- Discussion of responsible directorship

- Overview of specific institutional strategies

- Overview of foundation strategies

- Overview of current priorities

- Briefings by the foundation staff

- Conversations with institutional leaders

- Campus tour

The best programs often schedule several sessions at convenient times during the first year for new members. This spreads out the information and provides more opportunities to engage and monitor the progress of the new members.

The first board meeting, and the subsequent first year of directorship, can determine a director's early effectiveness and long-term success. Carefully consider the new director's committee assignments. Some boards invite new members to sit in on all committees during their first year. Also, ensuring that the new director is socially integrated typically is the responsibility of the mentor; this means making introductions, engaging in conversations, and offering other entrees to the social culture of the board.

Consider developing a new director's "toolbox" — a simple, indexed loose-leaf notebook. It might contain the following:

- An annual schedule of board meetings and events that directors should commit to their calendars;

- Fact sheets about the foundation and institution with suggested answers to frequently asked questions;

- Information about each school and program within the institution;

- Bulleted references to institutional priorities and strategic plans;

- Directories of foundation board members and staff, the institution's trustees or regents, and officers of the alumni association;

- Tips on prospecting or preparing for fund-raising calls;

- Standard forms and guidelines commonly used by all directors;

- Miscellaneous and occasional items that keep the director informed about the board, the foundation, and the institution; and

- Any other materials your board members have found helpful.

6. **Assess director performance.** No other responsibility of the committee so tests its image with the board. Director performance assessments must be seen as fair, objective, and untainted by board politics. The process must be carefully constructed to fit each board's culture, but attention to a few basic principles is useful:

    Fair and measurable criteria. Some boards keep the criteria short and simple: a minimum attendance rate, active participation in the work of the board, and follow-through on philanthropic responsibilities. One option is to use a "director report card," a self-reporting mechanism. (See the sample "Foundation Director Report Card" at the end of this chapter.)

    A known and routine assessment schedule. Two assessment points are appropriate: at the end of the first year of directorship and in the final year of the director's current term. At the end of the first year, find out whether the new director feels involved and committed. Does he or she have any ideas for how the board can do a better job? Any thoughts about future committee assignments? Is the board making the fullest possible use of the director's talents and experience?

    In the end-of-term assessment, directors should have the same opportunity to express satisfaction or concern about their own performance and that of the board. The committee should use this assessment to help reach an objective conclusion about renominating the director for a succeeding term.

7. **Decide whether to renominate sitting directors.** This is one of the most difficult and sensitive committee responsibilities. The tools with which to arrive at dispassionate judgments have been identified: (1) the board composition plan, (2) the criteria of director attributes, and (3) the results of the performance-assessment process. Failure to apply rules that govern director tenure uniformly and evenhandedly can erode the trust that binds board members, create a culture of ins and outs, and demoralize the board. The obstacles to achieving this level of apolitical discipline often stymie board leaders. Refuge in retirement policies — some form of term limits, for example — is a common solution.

8. **Anticipate future board leadership.** Monitoring the performance of new directors helps mark leadership potential. Performance assessment can focus on testing the willingness and readiness of sitting directors to move into leadership positions. The committee can influence the quality of future board leadership when it charts chair rotations of standing committees, appoints committee vice chairs, appoints leaders of ad hoc committees, and nominates vice chairs of the board.

9. **Motivate directors.** Directorship has evolved from an ill-defined avocation into a demanding, time-consuming commitment. Remember, however, that directors serve without pay and provide an irreplaceable resource for the institution. They want to make a difference in the future of the institution and improve the quality of life for individuals touched by the institution.

   The committee should function as a barometer of the board's morale. Generous recognition of exceptional service during a director's tenure should be a regular practice. Make it personal (board chair to director), and when appropriate, make it public (before the full board and the professional staff). And when directors retire from the board, mark the occasion with oral praise, written citations, and symbolic retirement gifts. The rewards of directorship are sometimes elusive and almost always intangible. Don't miss opportunities for recognition; it motivates the entire board.

10. **Develop programs that continue the commitment of former directors.** Directors devote years of their time and generous portions of their personal wealth. They do this because they feel connected to the foundation and the institution — physically, intellectually, and emotionally — through the exercise of their responsibilities. It makes good sense for the institution to find ways to cement these relationships when directors retire from board service. Two programs can meet this objective: an emeritus class of former directors and special programming for these individuals. The ideas are endless; the only principle to keep in mind is that former directors are a resource that deserves sustained cultivation. Such programs, which in some sense are beyond the purview of the committee on directors, may be best handled by another designated committee or task force.

53

Committee Structure

Committee size. In addition to ex officio members, a committee size of five to seven usually can do the job.

Rotating the membership. Don't let the committee become an unchanging enclave of director privilege. Without compromising the criteria for membership, cycle directors on and off the committee to ensure a balance between desirable continuity and fresh perspectives.

Frequency of meetings. The work and responsibilities of the committee require time and energy. For committees engaged in the early stages of developing strategies, policies, and practices, six meetings a year might be the minimum. Once protocols are in place, quarterly meetings should suffice. These can be a combination of meetings held contiguous with regular board meetings and sessions conducted by telephone or online.

Meeting agendas. A typical agenda should reflect the committee's responsibilities and include such topics as board composition, the process for bringing forward director candidates, orientation, and director performance assessments.

Reporting to the board. Much of the committee's work deals with confidential and privileged information. However, it is a mistake to allow the committee to become a "mystery" to board members at large. The committee chair, in addition to reporting to the board about such topics as the future direction of the board's composition and the conduct of director performance assessments, should find regular opportunities to inform the board about the committee's current priorities.

Policies and Practices

The policies and practices recommended by the committee on directors play a significant role in shaping the culture of the board and its environment for effective directorship. The issues raised below are framed as questions to consider; there are no right or wrong answers. What the committee concludes and recommends should be reflective of each board's distinct culture.

1. **Should the committee recommend director term limits?** Best practices from AGB suggest that term limits generally benefit all boards by regularly refreshing the board's talent base. Does the political will exist to execute a

term-limit policy with discipline, fairness, and uniformity? Does a mandatory rule cause more problems than it solves? Are there alternatives to term limits?

2. **Should the committee recommend shorter or variable terms?** Is the average term length of four years the best practice? Do virtually automatic renewals for successive terms create expectations that do not serve the board well? Would ascending terms — two, three, then five or perhaps two, four, four — encourage earlier and more effective discipline in performance assessment?

3. **Should the committee recommend a policy for individual director philanthropy?** Should policy guidelines be general and philosophical, or should expectations for giving be specific and quantitative? What belongs in a policy statement, and how much should be left to customized conversation with each director?

55

4. **What should be the committee's policy position on ex officio board members?** Should the institution's president be an ex officio member? With or without voting privileges?

5. **Should the institution's governing board members be candidates for foundation directors?** Are the pros of connecting the foundation to the institution offset by the cons of constricting the committee's flexibility to fill open foundation seats with broad and diverse talent? Can "connectedness" between the institution and foundation be achieved in other ways?

6. **How about ex officio members of board committees?** Should the board chair and chief executive be ex officio to all committees? What about other officers?

7. **How can the committee motivate underperforming directors?** How soon should a committee member or the chair meet with a director who has not been engaged or who is becoming a negative influence? Individuals have different styles, but when a member obviously is not fulfilling his or her responsibilities or is becoming a negative force, the committee should act. A member or the chair should meet with the director privately to determine whether there was a misunderstanding about expectations, problems with committee assignments, or a change in attitude toward the board or in his or her personal situation. If it is agreed that the person wants to continue, the two should develop a plan to help work through the issues. If not, the member may wish to resign, become officially inactive, or decline to stand for another

term. Failure to intervene with underperforming directors can lead to larger problems within the board.

Conclusion

The work of the committee on directors shapes the character and culture of the foundation board. For no other committee of the board is there this same intensity of mission focus, one that weaves the strategic responsibilities of the foundation together with the selection, training, and organizing of the foundation's directors. There is no single model for the committee on directors, but there are important principles in play. Getting it right from the outset is essential to building and sustaining the committee's level of trust with the board. If the committee fulfills its responsibilities with excellence, it will leave a legacy of sound mission stewardship and exemplary board leadership.

CASE STUDY: THE PIVOTAL COMMITTEE IN A BOARD'S EVOLUTION

In a time of transition, our university established a task force on board development. We had a new university president and were looking ahead to our first capital campaign. We needed to expand geographically and financially. With much more to do, we needed more people on the board. Our task was to recruit a top-notch cadre of volunteers.

The nominating committee was the predecessor of our committee on directors, and a task force was the impetus to reorganize and expand the committee's responsibilities. The committee comprises a chair, vice chair, and seven members, plus the board chair and vice chair as ex officio members. The progress made by this committee has helped us evolve into a more stable and mature organization, a necessity as we moved from managing $5 million to more than $100 million.

Selecting new board members can be likened to acquiring a handful of sticks. Each criterion is a stick — and the idea is to grab as many as possible in each candidate. In all, the objective is to recruit people who can make the greatest contributions to the workings of the board and the foundation. No one individual will meet all the criteria. Here is a list that works for us:

- Commitment to institutional programs — that is, to this college or university and to the foundation;

- Willingness to give *priority* time to this cause;

- Potential for substantial financial support — giving and getting;

- Influence with others;

- Having a degree from this institution;

- Previous giving of time and money;

- Family and/or business connections with the institution;

- Ability to work with other volunteers and with staff;

- Characteristics that balance the board, whether in age, gender, geographic region, ethnic or racial diversity, or professional expertise.

Leadership potential

Of help in the recruitment process is a matrix or spreadsheet of board membership, tracking the various qualities and qualifications needed for an effective board at this stage of institutional development. (See "Board Composition Worksheet" at the end of this chapter.)Ball State Foundation also reviews attendance records, especially in drawing up recommendations for officer nominations.

In addition, we recommend keeping a prospect book with biographical data about potential nominees. Suggestions from all sources can be compiled, added to, and deleted from during the committee's deliberations. The committee on directors meets three times per year, in conjunction with full board meetings. Between meetings, the bio book serves as a reference and can be updated and annotated.

Committees on directors occasionally can expect to receive "rush" nominations — from the institution's president, for example. These instances require tactful handling. The committee should take the time for its normal procedures — personal contact, discussion of expectations, and so forth — so that its responsibilities are not circumvented.

The guiding principle on board appointments, regardless of board size, is that each seat should hold a worthy occupant who carries his or her weight and does the work. That is, in these times when

57

58

there is serious work to do, boards have no room for deadwood. The situation is most awkward if the board or the organization outgrows someone's interest. Term limits are a help. Our chairmanship began without term limits. For a young foundation, longer terms may be advantageous — in fact, needed — so that as the mission evolves, the organization has steadiness and continuity in its leadership. Arbitrary rotation of officers, before a pipeline of informed volunteers has had time to develop, may be counterproductive.

Our chairmanship eventually went to a three-year term, and now it is two years. Board members serve three-year terms, with a maximum of 12 years total. These changes reflect the evolution and maturation of our board and organization. The current arrangement also gives more board members the opportunity to assume major responsibility for the foundation.

Exposure to other institutional foundations, as well as lengthening experience, teaches that no single plan is entirely correct. What is right and timely depends on the foundation and the institution it serves. The size and nature of the college or university rightfully influence the shape of the foundation. Frankly, personalities too, are involved. Leadership relationships shape the workings of the foundation and its board. It is very important that the foundation board chair knows and works well with both the institution's president and the foundation's chief executive. Further, the foundation directors need to know and be able to work with the institution's governing board. The starting point is the committee on directors, where board recruitment and development begin.

By recruiting and engaging strong board members, the committee on directors ensures a strong future for the institutionally related foundation. A strong board with strong leaders can be a worthy partner for its institution.

J. Richard Marshall
Chairman Emeritus, Ball State University
Foundation Board and former chair of its
committee on directors.

BOARD COMPOSITION WORKSHEET

	Current Board Profile	Last Class Elected	Ideal Next Class	Ideal Profile in 5 years
Age				
70 and over				
60-69				
50-59				
40-49				
30-39				
Under 30				
Gender				
Male				
Female				
Ethnicity				
White				
African American				
Asian American				
Latino/Hispanic				
Native American				
Other				
Area of Expertise				
Business				
Education				
Government				
Health/Medical				
Technology				
Executive Management				
Entrepreneur				
Finance/Investments				
Legal				
Marketing/PR				
Fund Raising				
Gift Planning				
Other				

60

BOARD COMPOSITION WORKSHEET
(continued)

	Current Board Profile	Last Class Elected	Ideal Next Class	Ideal Profile in 5 years
Geographic Distribution				
Southeast				
Northeast				
Midwest				
Northwest				
Southwest				
Institutional Relationship				
Alumni				
Parent				
Faculty/Staff				
Friend				
Other Boards				
Advisory Councils				
Awards				
Other				
Length of Service on Board				
Over 10 years				
5-10 years				
2-5 years				
one year or less				
Other				
History of Giving				
Annual				
Campaign				
Special projects				
Other				
Director, Public Corporations				
Director, Private Foundations				
Elected Official				

FOUNDATION DIRECTOR REPORT CARD

[Adapted with permission of the East Carolina University Foundation]

The foundation's mission is to raise, manage, and distribute private resources for the benefit of students and the university. Our work constantly improves the quality of the university and heightens its prestige. When we joined the board, we acknowledged a set of expectations that described minimum levels of involvement. The committee on directors thought a periodic self-review of our activities would be helpful. Your thoughts about the process will be welcomed. Please complete and return to the committee on the directors in the attached envelope.

Sincerely,
(Committee Chair)

Directions: Please indicate your responses in the column(s) to the right of each item, using a "Y" (yes), "N" (no), or "P" (pending). Please address any comments or notes for follow-up in the "Notes" panel, indicating the item number and your thoughts.

Meeting / Event Attendance	Yes	No	Pending
1. Attended board meetings			
• Fall			
• Winter			
• Spring			
2. Attended committee meetings			
• Meeting			
• Meeting			
• Meeting			
3. Attended new member orientation session			
4. Attended other university-sponsored events			
• On campus (list favorites)			
• Off campus (list favorites)			

FOUNDATION DIRECTOR REPORT CARD
(continued)

Foundation Participation / Support	Y	N	P	Contact Me
5. Made annual gift to academic programs, Chancellor's Circle, or Foundation Fellows				
6. Made a gift to the current major campaign				
7. Served as a campaign volunteer in a leadership position				
8. Included the university in my estate plan				

Gift Solicitation / Stewardship	Y	N	P	Contact Me
9. Identified and informed staff members of potential prospect(s) for gifts				
10. Made solicitation call(s) individually or with another board member/university representative				
11. Actively cultivated potential donor(s) and/or participated in stewardship of donor(s)				
12. Set up gift-cultivation calls for university staff/volunteers				
13. Wrote personal letters/notes to acknowledge gifts				

FOUNDATION DIRECTOR REPORT CARD
(continued)

University Promotions	Yes	No	Pending

14. Provided information to other individual(s)
    or firm(s) concerning:
    - Admissions
    - Scholarship campaign
    - General questions/interest
    - Gifts
    - Programs

15. Sought additional information on
    campus programs/events

Other Activities	Y	N	P	Contact Me

16. Hosted an event in home,
    club, or other venue

17. Thanked a faculty member,
    staff member, or volunteer
    for excellent work

18. _____

19. _____

20. _____

**What can we do to improve your experience or the
overall effectiveness of the board?**

_____

_____

_____

The Executive Committee

Richard T. Ingram

T he executive committee often is pivotal to the effective functioning of the foundation board and can be enormously helpful to the board chair and chief executive as they fulfill their leadership responsibilities. Because the executive committee is the only committee vested with broad authority by the board itself (except for certain powers the bylaws properly reserve for the full board), how the committee applies its delegated authority requires careful attention.

Although the executive committee generally has the legal authority to act on behalf of the full board, it should use this authority only in genuine emergencies such as when the full board cannot be convened quickly. Rather, it is in other domains that the committee can be enormously helpful to foundation leadership — both board and senior staff officers.

By and large, foundation boards with fewer than 15-20 directors do not find an executive committee necessary. Recent AGB surveys reveal that the average number of directors on foundation boards is about 27. Executive committees typically are found to be part of committee structures in boards of this size.

Committee Charge

The executive committee's responsibilities should be articulated in the board's bylaws. These responsibilities and functions often describe what the committee is not empowered to do, rather than the other way around. That is, most bylaws stipulate that the committee can do virtually anything the board ordinarily is legally empowered to do *except* for specific matters reserved for the board itself. Articulating the committee's responsibilities in this manner misses an opportunity to take greater advantage of the committee's potential service to the board and its leaders.

The *board's* "reserved powers" typically consist of the following:

- Appointment and dismissal of the foundation's chief staff executive (except where this decision is shared with or belongs exclusively to the college or university chief executive);

- The sale or other disposition of real estate (if the foundation is separately incorporated) and other assets within its legal control;

- Election of foundation directors and board officers;

- Approval of its annual operating budget; and

- Amendment of its bylaws.

Although these powers are reasonable and appropriate, some boards may stipulate others, as may the terms of their "Memorandum of Understanding" with the host institutions. At the same time, however, it is important for the committee to retain significant authority to act for the board, provided everyone understands that such powers should be used only in exceptional circumstances.

The following language may be adapted for inclusion in bylaws to help clarify the committee's scope of responsibility:

> The executive committee's primary purpose is to help the board function efficiently and effectively. Its broad authority shall be used only as necessary and appropriate on matters that cannot or should not be delayed until the board's next regularly scheduled meeting or until a special meeting of the board should be called as specified in these bylaws, unless the board has specifically delegated it to do otherwise.

> The committee's primary charge is to serve as a "sounding board" for the chief executive and board chair to help set board meeting agendas, oversee progress toward goals articulated in board-approved planning documents, oversee the process by which the chief executive's performance is reviewed and compensation adjustments are determined, handle certain routine business to conserve board meeting time, periodically assess how board committees are functioning, and act on other matters assigned or delegated to it by the board.

> The executive committee shall have authority to act on behalf of the board on all matters except for the following, which shall be reserved for the board as specified elsewhere in these bylaws: selection and termination of the foundation's chief executive; selection of board members and board officers; amendment of bylaws; changing the foundation's statement of mission and purpose.

Committee minutes shall be sent to all trustees within 30 days of its meetings. Any formal actions taken by the committee shall be ratified by vote at the board's next regularly scheduled meeting.

Committee Structure

These four rules of thumb suggest the need for balance in meeting the executive committee's responsibilities:

1. The committee should have a membership of approximately one-third the size of the board itself.

2. The committee should be composed of the board's officers (typically the chair, vice chair, secretary, and treasurer) and the chairs of standing committees. Ideally, at least one or two executive committee positions should be "at large." Holders of these at-large positions should be annually nominated by the appropriate board committee and elected by the board along with the annual election or reelection of board officers. In addition, the committee on directors should review the executive committee's composition annually to ensure a reasonable balance between the need for continuity and the need for periodic rotation of at least some of its members.

3. The board chair should also chair the executive committee. (Some organizations have experimented with other arrangements, usually with disappointing results.)

4. The committee should meet often enough to conduct necessary business *between* regular board meetings, not in conjunction with them, but not so often as to intrude on the board's responsibilities. A board should guard against inadvertently abdicating its responsibilities to the executive committee. Such a practice is harmful to the full board's effectiveness if it suggests that two classes of directors exist — those who are on the executive committee and those who are not. Of course, the committee should only meet as often as necessary to discuss substantive matters, more often in a consultative capacity rather than in a decision-making capacity.

Committee Responsibilities

The executive committee has unique opportunities to influence how the board conducts its business. The duties this committee assumes will differ somewhat according to the particular foundation's committee structure, but the work of the executive committee should address the following:

- Significant matters that cannot wait for a scheduled board meeting.

- Matters referred to the committee by the board for study and possible resolution.

- Matters generated by the committee itself, especially those emerging from ongoing standing committee work at the request of the chief executive or board chair.

- Routine or relatively inconsequential matters requiring pro-forma action by the committee to conserve the board's time (though such items are more appropriately handled by the use of consent agendas at regular board meetings).

- Ways to help the chief executive and board chair identify issues and plan agendas for subsequent board meetings. In effect, the executive committee can serve as a steering committee for the full board. Ideally, most activities relating to the business of the board are handled by the board at large, especially through its various committees. However, some areas of business may be rare enough that no standing committee either exists or is needed; entrepreneurial or other nontraditional business opportunities fall into this domain.

- Matters that bear on assessing overall board performance. In concert with the chief executive and the various committee chairs serving on the executive committee, the chair should ask questions such as these:

  - Is attendance at board and committee meetings consistent? If not, why, and what can be done to improve participation?

  - Is the committee system working well? Which committees seem to be productive, and which do not? Why?

  - Are board and committee meeting agendas and supporting materials substantive and timely? Are meetings interesting and conducted effectively? Do our board colleagues depart meetings with a sense of accomplishment?

- What can be done to promote better communication between standing committees on issues of joint concern? Should some committee meetings be held jointly from time to time?

- Are adequate in-service education opportunities provided to broaden board member knowledge of institutional and foundation characteristics and higher education trends, as well as the expectations for board service? Is the orientation program for new foundation board members effective?

- Is it time for a board retreat to discuss the new and developing challenges confronting the institution or the foundation? Is it time to conduct a comprehensive self-study of the board's performance with third-party help?

69

Committee Effectiveness

Greater candor often prevails in executive committee meetings than in full board meetings, where members may be more reserved, feel more constrained, or be less candid. The foundation's chief executive and board chair should ensure, however, that the executive committee does not assume responsibility for matters that more properly lie within the purview of other standing committees — or the full board.

The executive committee's real value rests mostly on its capacity to serve as a sounding board for the foundation's volunteer and staff leaders, to function as a planning committee to track progress on agreed-upon goals, and to monitor the foundation chief executive's performance and compensation. On these matters and others like them, of course, the committee is accountable to the full board. Some questions to consider:

- **Does the executive committee effectively serve as a sounding board for the chief executive and board chair?** Consistent with the concept that the executive committee oversees the foundation's planning process, the chief executive should take to the committee new policy issues that have the potential to affect the foundation and, by extension, its host institution. In this capacity, the executive committee helps the chief executive adhere to the dictum of "no surprises." Further, the committee serves as a safe haven where new ideas can be tested and explored before they are taken to the full board or assigned to a standing committee for further study.

  By routinely introducing potential initiatives to the committee, the chief executive can only enhance his or her position on key issues. Winning early, albeit tentative, support from the board's leaders enables the chief executive to test assumptions, consider options, or prepare a stronger case before a matter is taken to the full board.

The board chair also can float ideas — for comment and reaction rather than necessarily for the committee's approval — before taking them to the full board. The strategy here need not be to request the executive committee's support or endorsement of an idea; rather, it may be to ensure that the best possible case has been prepared before bringing an initiative to the full board or to the appropriate standing committee for discussion, disposition, or resolution. Again, it is wise to avoid the perception that the committee is deciding on a course of action on the board's behalf.

- **Does the executive committee appropriately serve as the board's mechanism for overseeing the foundation's planning process and reviewing progress toward goals and objectives?** Having standing committee chairs serve on the executive committee with the board's officers allows coordination of ongoing committee work, thereby reducing the likelihood of duplication. It also enables the executive committee chair to assign sensible divisions of labor while culling the best and most timely information for discussion of major policy issues.

  The conventional and still appropriate wisdom is that boards do not *conduct* planning; rather, they insist that good planning be done by those who are best qualified to do it — the foundation and institutional staff. But foundation board members should participate in planning processes if they are to accept ownership of resulting goals and objectives. Board members can provide valuable expertise and insights from the larger community on many perplexing issues confronting the foundation's future. Ultimately, the foundation's planning priorities should reinforce and be consistent with the institution's priorities, planning process, and goals. The executive committee's responsibilities may obviate the need for a separate planning committee or may put it in the best position to determine when an ad hoc planning group should be convened.

- **Does the executive committee monitor the chief executive's performance, morale, health, and compensation?** Effective executive leadership can be nurtured only if it is recognized and supported by the board's leaders. The board chair, of course, should be the chief executive's primary partner in his or her relationship with the board. Sometimes a small compensation committee (whether standing or ad hoc) handles annual reviews of the chief executive's performance and compensation. Indeed, the executive committee may provide the chief executive with helpful advice and counsel when it is needed throughout the year — not simply at performance and compensation review times. Executive committee members are in the best position to monitor the chief executive's strengths and needs, to prevent small problems from becoming larger ones. Constructive and continuing feedback benefits everyone.

Periodically, the committee (or more likely, a subset of members) should discuss privately with the chief executive such matters as personal financial planning, professional development opportunities, vacations, corporate directorship opportunities, and various other matters of a personal or professional nature.

71

- **Are the members of the executive committee mindful of their responsibility to limit decision making to emergency situations except on matters clearly delegated by the full board?** This question needs little elaboration except to offer the reminder that what constitutes a genuine emergency is likely to differ among board members. This is a judgment call by the board chair and chief executive. Regardless, the committee should have authority to act on the board's behalf in adverse or emergency situations that might arise.

Finally, committee minutes should always be prepared and mailed to all board members within 30 days. The board chair and chief executive should keep the board informed of its doings, including the outcomes of the chief executive's performance and compensation reviews.

Some Closing Issues

Several issues are not addressed in this chapter because they may apply only to certain foundation settings or to the board's unique traditions. For example:

- Should all directors be made to feel welcome to attend and participate in executive committee meetings?

- Are the same trustees serving on the committee for extraordinary periods of time?

- For institutions that have a regional or national reputation and draw their students and foundation board members from a wide geographical area, how can the board avoid the tendency for local directors to dominate seats on the executive committee?

This list could be extended, but the point is clear: *The full board* should decide how it expects the executive committee to conduct itself. The board must clarify the committee's responsibilities and hold it accountable through the board chair and chief executive. This committee, which should convene no more often than the full board meets annually, holds great promise for helping the full board function effectively and responsibly.

The Finance Committee

Marcia G. Muller

T he finance committee is one of the primary board standing committees, second only to the executive committee in importance. By virtue of its charge, the finance committee's work touches on that of virtually every other board committee. The importance of the finance committee is especially prominent today, as the financial challenges (and controversies) facing institution-related foundations are more complex than ever.

Responsibilities of the Finance Committee

The finance committee provides oversight for all aspects of the foundation's finances and is central to the foundation board's fiduciary responsibilities. Depending upon the size, maturity, and degree of autonomy of the foundation, the list of specific responsibilities of the finance committee varies among boards. Standard bylaws of a foundation might include the following language (this is taken from the Wright State University Foundation Code of Regulations) to help distinguish the committee's charge:

> The finance committee shall include at least seven directors, including the corporation's treasurer. The committee oversees all aspects of the foundation's finances, including, but not limited to, preparing and submitting an annual budget to the full board for approval; monitoring the performance of the budget; reviewing the actions of the chief financial officer and his or her subordinates; and developing, in concert with other board committees and the institution, short-term and long-term financial benchmarks and strategies to promote the fiscal health of the foundation and the institution it supports.

The primary responsibilities of a foundation's finance committee are the following:

- Monitor the foundation's operating budget, including annual and long-range financial needs.

- Establish foundation financial priorities.

- Work collaboratively with other standing committees (the development and investment committees, for example) on responsibilities related to foundation finances.

- Ensure the accuracy of the foundation's financial records and their timely presentation to the full board.

- Assume responsibility for capital budgets (and debt-financing plans) and submit both to the full board for approval.

- Assist in efforts to protect donor rights and privacy.

74

- Inform the full board of the foundation's financial condition on a regular basis.

Foundation Operating Budget

All foundation finance committees must approve and monitor the foundation's annual operating budget. Foundation budgets incorporate most financial issues that are of concern to the entire board. In analyzing sources of revenue and budgeting for expenses, the finance committee encounters key policy and planning issues.

The revenue-generating opportunities for the funding of foundation operations are affected significantly by the foundation's financial relationship to its host institution. Endowment administrative fees, the use of short-term earnings on current funds, and consideration of gift taxes on incoming gifts are all sources to consider. Some foundations also look for entrepreneurial opportunities that might provide enhanced revenues for foundation operations and institution priorities. In any case, the finance committee is the appropriate starting point for recommendations, whether they maintain, modify, or add to sources of revenue.

On the expenditures side of the ledger, however, how much should be earmarked for general foundation administrative expense? And what should be allocated back to the university for cost-sharing reimbursement, special projects, scholarships, or discretionary funds for key administrators? Development staff members generally are paid through the university, where benefits and retirement programs also originate, and interdependent foundations frequently reimburse their institutions for all or part of salary and benefit costs. Independent foundations, on the other hand, assume responsibility for funding all staff salaries and benefits, office expenses, and all other foundation-related expenses. Support of campus department-assigned fund-raisers is an appropriate expense for negotiation with the institution, although independent foundations currently are assuming greater responsibility for funding these positions. Salary decisions for the foundation's chief executive and other key staff require significant attention from the finance committee of interdependent foundations, again, depending on whether foundation staff are supported fully or in part by state funds.

Many foundations also provide university presidents with partial support for compensation packages, along with automobiles, contributions for housing (especially relative to a president's fund-raising responsibilities), club memberships, travel for spouses, and other perquisites that are beyond the budget parameters or policies of public institutions. Foundation support for presidential compensation packages is growing increasingly controversial. Finance committees should consider, along with the full board, whether such practices should be maintained going forward. Foundation boards can be a voice in support of states' footing the full cost of chief executive compensation packages.

In cases where state policies regarding presidential salaries make foundation supplements almost a requisite to attracting quality leadership, the committee should consider a policy that facilitates an efficient process of moving funds from the foundation to the institution. The foundation should not seek to influence the allocation of those targeted funds once the transfer takes place.

A hypothetical checklist that summarizes foundation budget considerations might look like the following:

- **Revenue Considerations**

    1. Endowed funds for foundation operations

    2. Unrestricted gifts

    3. Administrative charges for endowment management

    4. Earnings on current funds

    5. Assessments to all gifts for support of fund-raising

    6. Unrelated business income

    7. Other, including privatization initiatives

- **Expenditure Considerations**

    1. Salaries and benefits

    2. Rent

    3. Professional service fees

4. Taxes on property held

5. Insurance

6. Meeting expenses

7. Fund-raising costs

8. Debt service

9. Salaries, benefits, and prerequisites

10. Reimbursements to university for cost-sharing agreements

11. Discretionary funds for university president and/or selected administrators

12. Grants to university programs/projects

13. Capital investments/expenditures

14. Other

While not every item on the checklist will apply to every foundation, it may suggest areas for further study or development.

Staff Responsibilities for Budget Management

Small interdependent or dependent foundations typically rely on an institutional officer (or in some cases, a foundation staff officer) to monitor overall financial progress through the foundation's fiscal year and to prepare the periodic consolidated financial statement and the foundation's statement of financial position. Large foundations usually have a staff officer, often the vice president for finance or a comptroller, who provides the committee with regular financial updates. Independent foundations have staff that focus solely on foundation finances.

While it is tempting to rely heavily on the reports, judgments, and advice of the financial staff team, finance committee members, as fiduciaries, must not abrogate responsibility for the oversight of the foundation's annual and long-term financial concerns. The committee, through its chair, is responsible for informing the full board about the financial condition of the foundation.

The Work of the Finance Committee

A Catalyst for Coordination

A broad interpretation of "all aspects of the foundation's finances" suggests that the finance committee take the lead in carrying out the board's primary responsibility for fiduciary oversight. Monitoring financial accountability is delegated by the board to the committee, although all directors hold legal responsibility as fiduciaries. The committee's mandate, therefore, revolves around the raising, managing, and distribution of funds. The overlapping responsibilities with other committees of the board have implications for donor relations, relations with the host institution, and the credibility and image of the foundation as a well-managed entity. Quite literally, "the buck stops with the finance committee."

Understanding University Finances

Armed with a working knowledge of university fiscal affairs and priorities, the finance committee can more intelligently address both short-term and long-term financial planning for the foundation. It is incumbent upon the foundation chief executive, the institution president, and the institutional chief financial officer to share critical and timely information with the committee on a regular basis. Regular financial updates help inform the foundation's advocacy role in articulating the need for private support.

77

Defining Priorities for Private Support

As public colleges and universities collectively grapple with shrinking state support, the foundation finance committee has a responsibility to assess the institution's immediate or short-term needs for private support — both traditional private support and alternative revenue sources. The strategically focused finance committee, working collaboratively with the foundation development committee, will help shape annual fund-raising targets for which the full board shares responsibility. Collaboration between these two committees can temper an idealized funding wish list with the realities of what projects or priorities are most marketable among donors and what amount is feasible from other private sources.

Once the annual targets for private support are agreed upon, the finance committee must help ensure that fund-raising costs are appropriately incorporated into the annual budget process. The degree to which foundations will bear these costs will vary among independent and interdependent foundations. However, the finance committee should work with the development committee and staff to monitor the costs associated with raising private support. Fund-raising costs, including those associated with planning and implementing a campaign, need to be appropriately planned and budgeted.

Long-Range Planning and Problem Solving. Beyond the financing of annual fund-raising costs, the finance committee should be an active partner in the development of a foundation's strategic plans, emphasizing the development of a realistic or even a "stretch" set of financial benchmarks for the foundation. The committee can help the full board understand the need for the foundation plan to mesh with the host institution's long-term priorities. It can help position the foundation for long-term and sustained success by developing policies and contingency scenarios that will ameliorate the effects of financial volatility and more effectively preserve the purchasing power of the endowment. Three specific areas in which the committee should provide some independent or shared leadership include:

78

1. **Reconsideration of the 5 percent endowment payout rate.** The 5 percent rolling average became the industry standard in the 1980s and 1990s. Institutions, foundations, and endowments may want to consider variables that might foster a change in the spending rate, especially in the face of inflated asset values that accrued during the bull market. Endowment spending rates, typically the responsibility of the investment committee should, perhaps, also be considered by the finance committee in the context of its long-range planning responsibilities. Conversations between the respective committee chairs, through the board's executive committee, might appropriately influence the asset-allocation and the endowment-distribution deliberations of the investment committee and vice versa.

2. **Building reserves.** Financial volatility has driven home the need for foundations to address the subject of building foundation reserve funds. In the 1990s, earnings in excess of the payouts and administrative fees provided a cushion. Newly formed endowment funds had no such accumulation of excess earnings for payout; some funds fell below their historic dollar value, forcing a temporary termination of payouts. The current review of the Uniform Management of Institution Funds Act (UMIFA) requirements should go a long way to protect against funds going "under water." However, scholarships, professorships, and programs that were unfunded cast a pall on the glow of fund-raising success that many colleges and universities enjoyed in the late 1990s. Angry and skeptical donors, alumni, and faculty blamed foundations for mismanagement or misrepresentation of success.

   The finance committee is responsible for addressing the subject of building reserves, which can buffer future earnings shortfalls or provide for special needs. A commitment to build reserves can be a joint effort with the host institution, or it can be undertaken independently by the foundation. Collaboration between the host institution and the foundation is preferable, particularly when the foundation has an interdependent relationship with the college or university.

3. **Attracting unrestricted gift funds.** The finance committee and the development committee can work together to define the need, articulate the rationale, and develop strategies to increase unrestricted funds for the foundation, which are always among the most challenging to raise. The long-term financial planning the finance committee oversees should aspire to generate greater unrestricted support. In this way, the finance committee and the development committee can forge a partnership that goes well beyond their more traditional and focused responsibilities.

   While foundation volunteers, like other donors, have specific philanthropic preferences, finance committee members should set an example by making their own unrestricted gifts in addition to supporting specific projects and campaign priorities. Ideally, the full board will follow suit in its own giving and advocacy.

Financing Campaigns

Fund-raising campaigns have become a permanent fixture in higher education. Every institution struggles with how to finance them, a task that foundations frequently are asked to undertake in whole or in part. The goals for campaigns have grown dramatically, and the commitment to raising significant support requires a corresponding investment.

   The finance committee is the logical place to address the funding issues associated with campaigns that may extend over a period of three to seven years. Will additional staff need to be hired? How will foundation annual operating budgets be affected by the demands of a campaign? What investments should the foundation make in improving information systems, evaluating gift potential among constituents, increasing institutional visibility, and donor cultivation? Should the foundation consider incurring debt to enable capital projects to be completed? What funding mechanisms should be considered in financing the campaign? Foundations that are not asked to share responsibility for planning, financing, and executing fund-raising campaigns will not be effective in carrying out their fund-raising mission.

Current Issues

New Approaches to Generating Revenue

Most foundations have sought to augment shrinking public support through philanthropy. However, traditional approaches to attracting private support are unlikely to make up for lost state revenues and expanding needs. The nontraditional and entrepreneurial approaches to revenue generation, addressed in detail in Chapter 4, may become increasingly common. For-profit ventures — bookstores, campus-based hotels and food franchises, real estate ventures, and other related endeavors — are being undertaken under foundation auspices. The finance committee must take a leadership role in determining the feasibility and advisability of such ventures and then ensuring that sound management structures and long-term financing, based on an approved business plan, exist to support new initiatives.

More Flexible Gift Agreements

Once upon a time, donors made gifts and pledges to foundations and other nonprofit organizations and rarely concerned themselves with how their contributions were invested or managed. Donors today are more likely to want active and ongoing input into these decisions.

The Wright State University Foundation recently received a multimillion-dollar gift to support a program that had been created by the donor's original seven-figure commitment. As an experienced investor, the donor wanted the earnings to accrue to the project in question but also wanted the gift to be completely spent down over the next few years. This posed a dilemma for the foundation because traditionally the earnings on nonendowed gifts support the foundation, not the project. The solution was to create a quasi-endowment that preserved the foundation's 1 percent administrative charge, provided earnings for the project, and carefully outlined annual access to the principal until the fund was depleted.

The University of Minnesota Foundation has been a pioneer in recognizing and addressing the need for greater flexibility in gift agreements to accommodate donor requirements. Finance committees need to be aware of the growing need for flexibility and be willing to work with the investment committee, the development or gift acceptance committee, and perhaps a planned giving committee in order to maintain prudent guidelines while meeting donors half-way. One size does not necessarily fit all donors, and it behooves the finance committee to incorporate various types of gift agreements among a foundation's financial policy statements.

Finance Committee Leadership

The chair of the finance committee should be a director who has sufficient experience on the board to be knowledgeable about the foundation's fiscal history, policies, procedures, challenges, and partnership with the host institution. The chair must be an effective communicator. Professional experience in financial management is an important asset, as is a reputation for impeccable integrity. The chair also must be free of conflicts that might call into question his or her recommendations and decision making.

The finance committee chair, along with board officers and standing committee chairs, should be a member of the board's executive committee. This assignment ensures that communication with other standing committees is formalized, that the fiscal stability and long-term economic health of the foundation has a central focus, and that the finance committee has a conduit to the full board for decision making beyond its scope.

The complex and changing issues of concern to the finance committee requires its chair to be a big-picture thinker, someone who is well respected by fellow board members, and an expert in the financial arena. While the finance committee chair's expertise implies an extended term in that position, good board practice suggests that both the finance committee and the committee on directors actively develop future prospective committee chairs, as term limits necessitate leadership changes throughout the board.

Finance Committee Composition

A foundation board's finance committee probably should include ten to twelve directors. In light of today's financial challenges and the committee's obligation for long-range planning, policy development, donor relations, and institutional relations, the committee needs a variety of expertise. Obviously, a basic understanding of higher education finance and financial statements is essential, but the committee's oversight responsibilities require diverse skill sets among its members. Valued expertise among committee members should include financial analysis and administration, institutional investments, and planning. Directors who are responsible for meeting a bottom line in their own professional fields will be appropriately focused on the committee's primary charge. Those directors with less formal expertise in financial matters also have a role, for they bring fresh perspectives and a willingness to ask unconventional questions.

Because the finance committee bears some responsibility to take a longer view — much like the investments committee — continuity is important. Ideally, the term of service should be three years (based on a model of a three-year board term) with the option of reappointment for a second three-year term on the committee. Preferably, no more than one-third of the committee should turn over in a given year.

Most foundation boards encourage directors to serve on more than one standing committee. It makes sense to include representatives from such committees as development and planned giving, real estate, investments, and strategic planning on the finance committee.

A major donor perspective should be represented on the committee, though one would hope that the foundation's strongest volunteers also would be among the institution's top donors. The inclusion of a faculty member or university administrator also is worth considering, but the decision to do so requires balancing foundation autonomy with the need to foster strong and trusting relations within the host institution. A core of institutional representatives who understand the complexities of a foundation's finances can be a positive move.

Staff support for the finance committee is critical. The foundation's chief executive officer and chief financial officer should be actively engaged with the finance committee. Where an interdependent model exists, representation from the host institution's business and finance office is also wise.

In simpler times, foundation finance committees generally were "approving" bodies, largely reactive in the conduct of their responsibilities. Today, finance committees are being asked to address a full range of financial and procedural policies as well as issues concerning institutional integrity and credibility.

Ensuring Integrity

As donors once made gifts with little thought as to the details of how their gifts were managed, they also were inclined to assume that high integrity levels prevailed in the management and stewardship of their gifts. A few, albeit well-publicized, scandals among high-profile nonprofits have created wariness among some donors, and corporate scandals have only compounded such concerns. Better Business Bureaus have tightened endorsement standards for nonprofits. All foundations need to be aware and sensitive to the need for greater accountability, transparency, and adherence to rigorous standards.

It used to be common for foundations to merge the finance and audit committees' responsibilities under one committee. With a brighter spotlight and demands for greater accountability for boards and directors, foundations increasing are separating these functions. Ensuring that the foundation's financial and business practices and staff oversight are beyond reproach now are the audit committee's purview. The finance committee has many more areas of focus today; it is neither appropriate nor practical to have a finance committee retain audit responsibilities as well.

Challenges Ahead

Finance committees will be asked to ensure that prudence prevails in the expenditure of unrestricted funds. This suggests that written spending policies applicable to unrestricted funds need to be in place. Such policies should protect the flexibility of foundation funds, while curbing excesses. In the wake of corporate scandals and in the spirit of the Sarbanes-Oxley Act, foundations will be challenged to adjust and fine tune that balance of healthy disclosure, reasonable discretion, and donor privacy.

Foundations are focused on raising private resources, managing assets, and building bridges to the broader community. Yet few have done a great job of interpreting to the community how the funds they have raised and shepherded have affected students. Finance committees are most effective when they can translate the impact of the numbers into actual lives touched and academic interests served. Effectively communicating such messages not only burnishes the foundation's image, but it also will link the foundation's mission more tightly to that of the host institution.

The Investment Committee

John S. Griswold, Jr.

There are two old adages that speak to the same subject from perspectives that are nothing less than polar opposites. I'm sure you're familiar with them: "God is in the details," goes one, while the other holds that "the devil is in the details." Whether divine or diabolical, investment committees of foundation boards must possess specialized knowledge and an ability to pay attention to detail.

This chapter examines several topics: the reason for having an investment committee, the basics of fiduciary obligations and applicable law, the responsibilities of the investment committee, methods of selecting members for service on the committee, and ways that the investment committee relates to the larger board. We'll also take a look at how various factors will lead to heightened challenges and a faster rate of change for investment committees.

Rationale for an Investment Committee

"Why have an investment committee at all?" is a question with multiple answers. In brief, the rationale for an investment committee is based on several factors:

Specialized skills, knowledge, and experience are required to manage an investment portfolio. Central to the foundation board's responsibility to manage the institution's endowment is the ability to manage long-term funds and provide appropriate oversight. The foundation board as a whole, however, cannot do the work of the investment committee, primarily because asset management requires highly specialized skills. Unlike most other committees (with the possible exception of the audit committee), investment demands a level of specialization, skill, and experience not required by most committees of the board.

Why have an investment committee when most boards have a finance committee? The finance committee is responsible for the overall financial well-being of the foundation, including its budget, operations, debt, short-term cash needs, and long-term capital projections. Its committee members require different skills and knowledge — such as accountancy — from those needed by investment committee members. To be sure, the finance and investment committees should communicate, but they are two essentially separate sets of governing functions.

A specific body within the board should take responsibility for developing and maintaining the guiding document of endowment management — the investment policy. A foundation's investment committee is responsible for crafting and implementing the investment policy, which serves as a roadmap to guide the foundation's investments in pursuit of specific objectives. The investment policy should be a written document that is shaped by the investment committee and approved by the full board. Investment policies are dynamic documents that should be subject to modification as needs and conditions change. While ongoing dialogue around the investment policy is healthy, committees should avoid constant change and revision in reaction to market conditions.

Investment committees are responsible for managing considerable sums of money. Notwithstanding the protracted and painful bear market of the early 2000s, endowments grew enormously over the course of the 18-year bull market that prevailed from 1982 until 2000. As a result, the stakes today are a lot higher than they were some two decades ago.

Public institutions supported by dedicated foundations increasingly rely on endowments. At most public institutions, the percentage of the institution's operating budget accounted for by the transfer of funds from the foundation has grown considerably. At 5 percent to 10 percent or more of the budget, the sums can be substantial.

Boards need to monitor and manage risk in a world in which financial markets can change rapidly. Risk tolerance varies greatly among higher education institutions. And while most people think in terms of market risk, there is a universe of risks that must be understood, measured, and monitored. A few include economic risk, inflation risk, geopolitical risk, credit risk, liquidity risk, concentration risk, and interest rate risk. Once again, this task requires specialized knowledge and experience.

Highly complex financial instruments (derivatives, for example) and investment strategies (such as hedge funds) underscore the need for specialized skills and knowledge within the board. Adoption of alternative investment strategies and asset classes that only the largest and most sophisticated endowments previously had used are now common. Hedge funds, absolute return and enhanced index strategies, venture capital, private equity, natural resources, and global private capital comprise increasingly larger shares of endowment assets. Today, the number of "plain vanilla" portfolios built around publicly traded stocks, bonds, and cash is shrinking, and portfolios that include allocations to alternative and private strategies are growing. This broad range of investment strategies and risk characteristics require not only professional-level competence but also a greater level of due diligence in order to be properly evaluated.

Responsibilities of a Fiduciary

The concept of intergenerational equity captures the essence of the fiduciary responsibility of an investment committee. The late Yale University economist James Tobin wrote that trustees "are the guardians of the future against the claims of the present." Thus, we should ask, "What is a fiduciary?" A basic definition is one who acts in a position of confidence or trust on behalf of another; surely, foundation directors are fiduciaries.

The first thing an investment committee member should understand and appreciate is the fiduciary's duties of care, loyalty, and responsibility. These are legal requirements of fiduciaries, and anyone who becomes one must adhere to those duties in service to a public-benefit corporation that receives a tax exemption and certain other dispensations from the government. The point is, the fundamental principles of higher education are rooted in legal, ethical, and moral responsibilities.

For foundation directors who serve on investment committees, the duty of loyalty is to avoid conflicts of interest and to be faithful to the foundation. The duty of care demands that investment committee members become well acquainted with all of the information and pertinent facts under the committee's purview. Financial or investment professionals bring useful backgrounds to the boardroom, but education becomes all the more crucial for those from outside those realms. Finally, the duty of responsibility is to maintain the policies of the foundation and to follow those policies in a disciplined and consistent manner.

Ultimate fiduciary responsibility still rests with the full board of directors. The investment committee should be responsible to the full board and report to it on a regular basis. Reporting should be done regularly and in layman's terms because the board members themselves, most of whom are not investment specialists, need to understand the principles behind the investment committee's thoughts and actions. Communicating effectively is one of the many key responsibilities of the committee chair.

Thirty or forty years ago, it was common for trustees or directors to manage endowment assets personally. Classical trust law held that a "trustee cannot properly delegate to another power to select investment." While legal questions about delegation existed as late as the early 1970s, the need for delegation was recognized because board members (volunteers) could not manage considerable sums of money on a part-time basis.

The concept of endowment dates back at least to the Middle Ages, when the term described the land donated by wealthy landowners to religious groups that used its rental income for financial support. Later on, as universities became established, donated land began to support secular programs. Over the centuries, endowments came to include not only land holdings but financial assets as well. The rules governing endowment use followed English trust law, which limited managers to investing only in securities appearing on court-prescribed lists. That changed in 1830, when the famous case of *Harvard College v. Amory* freed trust managers from the requirement of using an approved list of investments. The case also established the "Prudent Man Rule," which essentially stated that managers were free to make any investment they thought wise as long as they did not exceed the bounds observed by a "prudent man."

For much of the 20th century, the "prudent man" invested the bulk of educational endowment funds in bonds and mortgages — fixed-return investments. It was not until after World War II that those investing for endowments entertained thoughts about equities, and even then the notion took hold very slowly. A major breakthrough came in 1972 with the introduction of the Uniform Management of Institutional Funds Act (UMIFA) and its eventual passage in the majority of the 50 states.

UMIFA established four key provisions: (1) Endowment funds could be pooled for investment purposes, similar to a mutual fund; (2) the Prudent Man Rule could be applied to the endowment as a whole and not each individual investment; (3) board members could delegate investment management responsibilities; and (4) capital appreciation could be spent without violating the prohibition against spending principal. This last provision gave rise to today's concept of "total return." It broadened the Prudent Man Rule to base decisions on the expected total return of the investment, with total return being defined as capital appreciation as well as income. (While most higher education institutions follow this approach today, boards are well advised to seek the guidance of legal counsel as to the specific limitations prescribed by the endowment for which they are responsible.)

It should be pointed out that with regard to the spending of restricted funds, UMIFA permits all funds — restricted and unrestricted — to be pooled and a single spending rate applied against the total; this eliminates the necessity of applying a spending rate against each restricted fund on an individual basis. Another question about spending that arises in the case of public institution foundations is whether operating costs should be included in the spending rate or should be a separate charge against the foundation. In my view, it can be done either way and is a matter of institutional preference, but from a cost-accounting standpoint, the best approach is to account for them separately.

(Readers should note that as of this writing, UMIFA is undergoing review and is likely to be modified sometime in 2006. The revised UMIFA likely will provide for more flexibility in spending decisions by boards.)

A Closer Look at the Investment Policy

89

Perhaps the most important job of the foundation board's investment committee is the development of the investment policy that it submits to the full board for approval. The pillars on which the policy is built include the following:

Objectives. What is the purpose of the endowment, and how does it support the foundation in support of the mission of the host institution? Before assets are allocated or investments selected, the committee — and ultimately, the full board — must be in agreement on the role of the endowment as it relates to the mission of the foundation and the institution. In the business world, objectives can be expressed in quantifiable and measurable terms — revenues, earnings, return on investment, or market share, for example. There is less opportunity for such specificity in the nonprofit world, including the higher education community. Thus, in setting endowment policy, directors first should understand the foundation's mission to provide support for its host institution's priorities. With this knowledge, they will be able to review the condition of the institution and its short-term and long-term needs.

Decision makers may feel that the endowment's objective should be expressed in terms of intergenerational equity, or they may decide that the objective is to grow the endowment. Once the direction is established, it will have major effects on decisions concerning spending policy and asset allocation.

Spending Policy. The key question for an investment committee is how much of the "true" or restricted endowment can be spent each year and still maintain the long-term purchasing power of the endowment. This is the crux of the concept of intergenerational equity. An important point to bear in mind: Spending policy and asset allocation are closely linked and must be compatible. The critical challenge for the committee is to establish a strategic asset allocation that will generate the returns necessary to support the agreed-upon spending policy at an acceptable level of risk.

Asset Allocation. In seeking the return the foundation needs to support its spending policy — once again, taking risk into consideration — the investment committee starts with its most crucial decision: how to balance the endowment portfolio among various asset classes. This is the cornerstone on which an investment policy is built.

History demonstrates that there are frequent and significant fluctuations in the returns of different asset classes. Diversifying across a range of asset classes helps dampen the impact of these swings. For much of the last century, diversification meant allocating funds among different stocks or bonds — in other words, diversifying within an asset class. But this changed in 1952 when Harry Markowitz, "the father of modern portfolio theory," developed the mathematical model that described the reduction in volatility that occurs when investment with different patterns of return are combined in a portfolio. Markowitz showed that the relative risk of a security should be viewed in the context of the entire portfolio. Thus, he refocused investors on the interrelationships among the classes of securities within a portfolio. This gave rise to the awareness that securities, potentially volatile on their own, could be combined to reduce the volatility of the overall portfolio as long as their returns are uncorrelated.

Correlation refers to how asset classes relate to each other — in other words, the degree to which asset classes move in tandem with or independently of one another. Investing in asset classes that can be expected to move together produces little diversification benefit. If asset classes are uncorrelated — for instance, small cap equity funds and real estate — the result is greater diversification and reduced overall portfolio volatility. As a point of reference, the *Commonfund Benchmarks Study* for the five-year period 2001-05 found the following average asset allocation for foundations affiliated with public higher education institutions or systems:

Type of Investment	2001	2002	2003	2004	2005
	%	%	%	%	%
Domestic equities	51	44	46	47	41
Fixed income	28	26	24	22	17
International equities	15	15	12	13	13
Alternative investments*	5	14	16	15	26
Short-term securities/cash	1	1	2	3	3

* Includes hedge funds, venture capital, private equity, equity real estate, energy and natural resources, and debt strategies.

Perhaps the most readily identifiable trend over this period is the threefold increase in the allocation to alternative investments. To fund this increase, there has been a modest reduction in domestic equities and a somewhat greater reduction in the fixed-income allocation.

Rebalancing. A foundation's long-term asset allocation (often referred to as the "policy allocation") should not be — and practically speaking, cannot be — rigid and inflexible. Owing to the varying rates of return produced by different asset classes, the policy allocation will be exceeded in some asset classes while others shrink. When this occurs, it is necessary to rebalance the portfolio back to the policy allocation. As a rule, most investment committees have a policy of rebalancing every six or 12 months, or other set time period. Rebalancing too frequently can be disruptive and costly, while rebalancing every two or three years incurs excessive portfolio risks.

One readily manageable approach to rebalancing is to establish a range or "bands" around the target percentage for each asset class in the portfolio. For example, a fixed-income policy allocation might be 20 percent of the portfolio. Under a banded approach, fixed income could increase to 25 percent or shrink as low as 15 percent. If either the upper or lower limit is breached, the allocation is returned to its target policy weight.

Manager Selection. Due diligence is conducted on a selected group of managers chosen by careful screening; these managers are monitored thereafter to ensure adherence to a chosen strategy and style. Managers should be studied in depth and selected not just for past performance but for their ability to complement one another in a diversified portfolio.

The decision to hire a manager involves both quantitative and qualitative considerations. Although performance is one factor in evaluating a potential manager, foundation officials also should be interested in the firm's investment decision-making process, senior management, ownership structure, internal controls, reporting, asset growth, and size (assets under management). In addition, officials should seek experience in differing investment climates and a clear investment philosophy and approach.

Once a manager is identified as a potential candidate, it is useful to evaluate the effect of the manager's inclusion in the portfolio using statistical risk/return measures, including standard deviation, alpha, beta, correlation, Sharpe ratio, and composite (simulated) returns to determine the appropriate policy weight of the potential manager. If the manager's style is a good fit for the fund, the committee will likely want to conduct on-site due diligence to review trading policies and risk-management procedures before making any commitment.

Several decision points are important in the process of hiring investment managers:

- **Diversification.** In diversifying the portfolio, consider manager styles and strategies in addition to asset classes.

- **Costs.** Check management, trading, and custody fees carefully; a foundation may incur relatively high costs and encounter high minimum investment requirements.

- **Performance analysis.** Monitor manager results individually, then combine for overall portfolio return. Measure a manager's performance against an appropriate benchmark and a universe of similar managers.

- **Service.** Be certain that the managers the committee recommends are prepared to meet the foundation's needs for information (otherwise known as transparency) and periodic portfolio review.

- **Fiduciary responsibility.** Directors and investment officers share responsibility for manager oversight. The full board of directors is responsible for approving overall investment policy, even though management of the funds may be delegated to the investment committee.

- **Ongoing monitoring.** Be certain that necessary controls and risk-management procedures are in place. This should include a periodic review of all internal policies and practices, as well as ongoing oversight of external investment managers to ensure compliance with written guidelines.

- **Operations capability.** The committee and board will want to be able to receive accurate current market values; the board will need a custodian to price securities in the portfolio.

Risk Management. Investment committees should think of risk as the possibility of failing to meet the board's investment objectives. Thus, it is important that every facet of a foundation's endowment management system, internal and external, is capable of recognizing and responding to risks. Bear in mind, risks should be measured and assessed in light of the committee's risk tolerance and return objectives (as all investing involves some level of risk).

Risk management is not a specific function but a discipline that pervades every facet of endowment management. It should be woven into every job description and every decision. Board members cannot implement effective risk-management practices themselves, but they should be aware of the issues surrounding risk management.

Sometimes, effective risk management is simply a matter of maintaining a healthy degree of skepticism and asking difficult questions: Is our portfolio strategy truly consistent with our stated objectives? In whose name are the assets in our portfolio held? Where are they held? Is the valuation accurate?

Asking uncomfortable questions is a good practice. If the board or staff does not have the wherewithal to define and develop an integrated risk-management capability it should seek consultative support at the outset.

Costs. The costs of a foundation's investment program can quietly undermine returns, especially in an environment in which lower returns are expected. Board and committee members must be certain that costs are being held to a minimum. The key issue is whether the same results are attainable at a lower cost. Expenses should be measured and controlled by negotiation and compared with those of peer foundations and institutions.

93

If an investment committee suddenly has discovered that costs have soared, it is likely that the committee has failed to exercise appropriate oversight. Cost control essentially involves three types of activity: diligent investigation of alternative management candidates, a tough approach to negotiating fees, and efficient oversight of the firms responsible for managing foundation assets. Cost control also means avoiding needless transactions, because every trading decision comes with a cost.

Despite the focus on controlling costs, balance and perspective are still needed. Directors do not want to compromise the effectiveness of a risk-management program, for instance, just for the sake of keeping costs to an absolute minimum.

Responsibilities. The board defines the responsibilities of all major participants in the endowment management process, starting with its own. One of its most fundamental responsibilities is the management of the endowment, an obligation it cannot delegate to external entities. The responsibilities of directors, the business or investment officer and staff, and any consultants should be defined in writing and clearly understood by all.

It is important to distinguish between investment policy questions that are appropriately delegated to the full board for review and approval and those that should remain with the committee. Clearly, the investment policy and its principal components need full board review. On the other hand, matters such as asset allocation and the retention or termination of specific portfolio managers are better left to the investment committee. It also is a good idea to have the foundation's general counsel review the policy to determine whether it conflicts with the state's version of UMIFA or other relevant statutes. (A sample foundation investment policy appears as Appendix D.)

Composition of the Investment Committee

Although the investment committee should include members who possess professional competence, individuals with unrelated experiences can bring important perspectives to the committee. Such individuals often serve as an effective sounding board; if they are uncomfortable with certain issues or policies, the full board is likely to be disquieted as well.

In addition, to broaden an investment committee's talent pool, it may be wise to recruit nondirectors. Doing so may help alleviate some of the inherent conflicts that arise among directors, and the practice provides an additional pipeline of prospective directors. The *2005 Commonfund Benchmarks Study* shows that nearly half of the participating foundations have nondirectors serving on their investment committees. At universities and colleges with the largest endowments ($1 billion or more), fully 71 percent have such individuals serving on the investment committee.

The committee chair. An effective chair is absolutely essential to the foundation investment committee. The chair of the full board should be certain that the investment committee chair is chosen very carefully. He or she should be an investment professional who fully understands the committee's charge and the needed balance among committee members. Among the chair's responsibilities are the following:

- Reporting to the board, since the board is the ultimate fiduciary;

- Recruiting and orienting new committee members;

- Establishing the structure for managing assets and reporting on performance;

- Balancing internal resources (for example, an internal investment office) and outside consultants, managers, and custodians;

- Maintaining a focus on the investment policy;

- Avoiding conflicts of interest, real or perceived; and

- Maintaining discipline in the committee's deliberations, so that all voices are heard and no single individual dominates the agenda.

Committee size. Six to eight members is about the right size for the investment committee. That makes it large enough to gain a variety of perspectives, to have a healthy mix of generalists and specialists, and to spread the workload so that one or two people are not overburdened. A committee of two or three is too small to achieve any of these attributes. A committee of twelve or more is too large and unwieldy and is inherently saddled with communication problems. The *2005 Commonfund Benchmarks Study* found that foundations have an average of 8.2 members on their investment committees — a slightly smaller average board size than the 8.6-member national average across all higher education institutions reported in 2004.

Foundations with the largest endowments (more than $1 billion) reported having an average of 10.5 committee members, whereas those with less than $10 million averaged 6.1 members. It may be the case that larger foundations desire committee members with specialized knowledge of alternative asset classes, such as hedge funds, absolute return strategies, venture capital, and private equity.

Length of service. An old joke says the longest tenured board members are on the investment committee, and the shortest tenured are on the long-range planning committee. It certainly is true that without term limits, investment committee members can become too firmly entrenched. Three consecutive three-year terms or two consecutive four-year terms is fairly common practice. It can take a couple of years for committee members to become entirely oriented, so a single three-year or four-year term can be too short; anything over eight or nine years total risks entropy. Rotation of members on and off the committee should be managed so that at any one time new members do not comprise more than one-quarter of the committee. The committee chair should be chosen from existing committee members; a committee member ending his or her first four-year term is an ideal candidate to become chair for a second and final term on the committee.

Committee meetings. The investment committee should meet three or four times a year. More frequent meetings can tempt committee members to micromanage and lead them to develop a short time horizon. However, committee members should make themselves available for interim conference calls dealing with urgent management decisions and should set aside time to read committee reports and recommendations.

Long-term matters — the overall investment policy, for example — may be reviewed once every two or three years, unless extenuating circumstances intervene. Asset allocation, however, should be reviewed at every meeting — not necessarily with the idea of making changes but to review how the portfolio is allocated at that time versus what the policy stipulates and to rebalance, if necessary. The meeting agenda also should include current and long-term performance data for each asset class, information that can be provided by staff or consultants. Sometimes, the agenda will include special items, such as capital campaigns or large gifts. Whether an upcoming meeting is viewed as special or routine, committee members should receive an agenda in advance. Minutes should be kept of all meetings for future reference.

On the matter of manager selection (and termination) committee members should not do the in-depth work on those decisions. Instead, they should act on recommendations of staff and/or consultants. (The only exception would be in rare cases in which the committee has neither staff nor consultants and the work, by default, falls to the committee, usually the chair.) Selecting investment managers is time-intensive and highly specialized work. There are thousands of managers from which to choose, and the process includes numerous steps: compiling a list of candidates, gathering information about them, narrowing the list, performing preliminary due diligence, selecting finalists, completing due diligence, hearing presentations, making the final selection, and negotiating terms.

Once hired, managers must be monitored on an ongoing basis, not only for performance but for any changes in management or structure, departure from investment guidelines, and other criteria. To be sure, committee members should question staff or consultants and carefully study their recommendations to fully understand the manager decisions they are asked to approve. But the all-important groundwork is delegated by the committee to staff and/or to consultants who have the required time, expertise, and experience.

Orienting new committee members is frequently neglected. The committee chair, perhaps with help from a consultant and the foundation's financial staff, should ensure an effective program is in place. An orientation session led by the committee chair, and ideally scheduled in advance of the first committee meeting of the fiscal year, should emphasize fiduciary responsibilities, foundation investment policies, and current issues before the committee.

What's Next for Investment Committees?

The work of foundation investment committees is becoming increasingly complex. These committees have access to many investment alternatives, most of which are in asset classes and strategies that are considerably less transparent and less easily understood than publicly traded domestic stocks and bonds. As a result, committees spend a good deal of time sifting through information.

The move to alternative investment vehicles will likely continue. The *2005 Commonfund Benchmarks Study* shows that the total percentage of assets allocated by foundations to alternatives has increased dramatically since 2000. If this trend continues, the issue of managers' capacity constraints will become more prominent. Consequently, as endowments grow, foundations are likely to hire additional managers, which will require more due diligence, monitoring, and risk management. Such expansions will place a greater burden on the investment committee. One way foundations are addressing these challenges is by recruiting nondirector specialists to serve on investment committees.

Foundation investment committees also may begin to take on more risk. It's an interesting phenomenon that when individuals who have become successful by taking risks become board members, they become far more risk-averse. This is both good and bad. Yet an endowment has an infinite horizon and can afford to take certain informed risks — such as liquidity risks — more easily than individual investors. Generally, taking more risk should mean higher rewards, so endowments should have an innate advantage over other investors.

It also may become more difficult to meet a committee's "bogey," or a return that equals or exceeds spending plus inflation plus costs. If returns regress to their long-term averages, we may endure a period of sub-par returns. Fortunately, inflation has been very low in recent years, though not as low for higher education, where costs include maintenance, salaries and benefits, and technology upgrades — a phenomenon measured by the Higher Education Price Index (HEPI).

Summary

In addition to investment expertise, foundation investment committee members need a broad understanding of the foundation and the host institution — their objectives and needs, their opportunities and limitations, and their long-term aspirations and past traditions. Directors should come to their committee positions with a fundamental grasp of the responsibilities of a fiduciary and an earnest desire to do what is right for the future of the institution they serve.

SPENDING: NO SINGLE ANSWER
TO ONE OF THE COMMITTEE'S TOUGHEST QUESTIONS

The two most critical issues facing investment committees are asset allocation and spending policy. Fundamentally, spending should be kept as low as possible — within reason. To spend 5 percent, a committee must believe its portfolio will return about 9 percent, factoring in roughly 3 percent inflation and another percentage point in costs. Nine percent returns may be optimistic, depending on the market, of course. Therefore, if long-term portfolio returns are in the 7 percent range, spending 5 percent will be problematic.

Committee members also should bear in mind that when it comes to payout rates, less ultimately becomes more. That is, when compared over 20 years, a spending rate of 4 percent will allow for greater capital accumulation in the endowment and greater cumulative spending than will a rate of 7 percent. This gives a foundation the ability to spend more in the future, while the higher spending rate actually reduces future absolute dollar spending.

Spending policies and practices vary considerably among education institutions, but the following are three widely used approaches:

- Spending a percentage of the market value of the endowment;

- Increasing prior spending by inflation; and

- Spending a percentage of a moving average of the endowment's market value — for example, the payout rate could be established at 5 percent of a three-year or five-year moving average of the endowment's beginning market value.

The *2005 Commonfund Benchmarks Study* of education institutions' investment policies and practices indicates that the vast majority follow the last approach. Some, however, are looking more closely at that spending approach and questioning whether it is best for the long term. The predetermined rolling three-year, 5 percent spending method seemed to work during the strong financial markets of the 1990s because it generated increases in spending amounts that far outstripped the rate of any measure of inflation. When spending rates are linked to declining market values, the opposite occurs, placing very real pressures on institutional budgets.

Had spending started at 5 percent and annual increases been based on price inflation (either the Consumer Price Index or the Higher Education Price Index) instead of inflated asset values, the spending would have been more sustainable. Now, however, it is becoming increasingly clear that the 5 percent three-year policy based on asset values led to overspending in the 1990s. Hence, it has created a threat to the concept of intergenerational equity. Many education institutions are already feeling pinched — and are confronting declining real spending — despite many years of strong stock market returns.

Considering that the two most important determinants of long-term return are asset allocation and spending rates, investment committees may want to reevaluate spending policies to identify a more appropriate long-term spending rate.

MISTAKES INVESTMENT COMMITTEES MAKE

Some of the more common pitfalls that can snare investment committees include the following:

Tactical mistakes

- Buying yesterday's winners

- Getting out of an asset class after it has fallen because it is "too risky"

- Buying something because you read about it in a business magazine (or anywhere else) or received a "hot tip" from a friend

- Averaging into a position over long periods of time in order to minimize the chance of a big mistake (either the position is right for the long term or it isn't)

Rebalancing mistakes

- Not having a disciplined rebalancing policy

- Postponing rebalancing decisions subject to market events

- Not using cash flows as an efficient means of rebalancing

Asset allocation mistakes

- Avoiding asset classes because of adverse prior experience of individual members ("I lost a bundle on X, and we shouldn't touch it!")

- Skewing the asset allocation because of a member's positive experience ("I've never sold a share of X, and I'm rich!")

- Not properly assessing the "riskiness" of individual asset classes versus the "riskiness" of the entire portfolio (avoiding "risky" asset classes, thus hurting the portfolio's overall risk-return characteristics)

- Confusing volatility with market direction (as in the 1990s when stocks only went up — therefore, they are not volatile)

Manager selection errors

- Chasing yesterday's winners

- Accepting someone else's word that a certain individual is a good manager instead of doing your fiduciary duty to kick the tires yourself

Spending mistakes

- Not having a spending plan that limits withdrawals in good times and prevents overspending in tough times

- Omitting "special" items that require withdrawals from the endowment from the spending total

Governance mistakes

- Micromanaging; for example, focusing on security selection or short-term performance

- Having too many investment committee members

- Not orienting new investment committee members

- Letting a strong-willed committee member dominate the committee's agenda

- Wasting time by straying from the agenda

The Audit Committee

Kevin Hoolehan and Larry S. Boulet

Not so long ago, it was widely assumed that all corporate, foundation, and governing board members were guided by honorable intentions. No one ever really thought to question their motives or actions. Today, however, board members of all types of organizations face unprecedented scrutiny. Although integrity certainly is expected of directors, few today assume that board members will always place the interests of the institution or organization above their own.

Alumni, faculty, students, parents, and the public demand financial accountability. Donors have exacting expectations for their invested funds. Government agencies ask probing questions about financial reports. The news media seek access to donor records. And everyone is shocked and angered over accounts of conflicts of interest and similar misdealing. These greater demands by constituents coupled with society's inclination to litigate just about any grievance are having far-reaching effects on higher education foundations and their directors.

This heightened visibility and the resulting potential for public humiliation have foundation board members wondering about their board service:

- Do our governance policies and organizational structure allow the board to monitor the foundation's operations effectively? Are the foundation's governance policies reviewed and changed as the foundation grows and changes?

- Does senior management set the appropriate "tone" for high standards of ethical business behavior?

- Do donors and other important constituents trust that information in our annual report accurately and completely reflects our financial condition?

- Will the foundation's internal control systems deter wrongdoing? Can its internal checks and balances detect errors that do occur?

- Are the foundation's management and staff adequately trained? Are they keeping up with new, complex regulations?

- Do we have potentially embarrassing conflicts of interest?

While an effective audit committee is not a panacea, it can help address such questions and mitigate the risks of embarrassment and reputational damage. Audit committees composed of talented, experienced, and diligent members who actively represent the interests of their fellow board members can provide the needed oversight to minimize risks and reassure directors that their fiduciary responsibilities are being fulfilled.

For donors and beneficiaries, the audit committee can provide a measure of confidence that the foundation's financial matters are appropriately and prudently addressed. For the foundation's management, the audit committee is a valuable resource of financial expertise and sound business judgment. By conscientiously carrying out their oversight and monitoring functions, members of the audit committee will help their board colleagues achieve a rare commodity — peace of mind.

When considering the audit committee's contribution to organizational governance, recent events in corporate America are instructive. An unprecedented series of corporate scandals shocked investors and weakened the public trust in some of our largest, most respected corporations, leading Congress to pass the Sarbanes-Oxley Act of 2002. In the public's mind, corporate boards shouldered much of the blame for falling asleep at the switch and failing in their fiduciary responsibilities.

In dealing with today's environment of heightened visibility and demands for greater transparency and accountability, boards of foundations can look to the Sarbanes-Oxley Act for guidance in quality standards for organizational governance. With its key focus on restoring investors' trust, Sarbanes-Oxley places a major emphasis on strong, active audit committees. Because the legislation considers audit committees a critical element of effective corporate governance, it establishes high expectations for such committees and high standards for their members.

Board members reviewing their foundation's governance structure and the role of an audit committee in light of Sarbanes-Oxley should consider several important strategic questions: Should we voluntarily adopt some of the best practices of Sarbanes-Oxley despite its limited formal applicability to nonprofit organizations? Should our audit committee's responsibilities go beyond monitoring the audited financial statements? What limits should we place on the audit committee's authority? There are tactical questions to consider as well: Should our audit committee be a separate, stand-alone committee or a subcommittee of the finance committee? To whom should our audit committee report — the chief executive or the board? What should we look for when recruiting and selecting audit committee members?

This chapter addresses these questions. In addition to the advice offered here, the mission, culture, and environment of each foundation undoubtedly will affect how foundation boards and executives answer the respective questions.

Committee Charge

The full board should agree on the scope and limitations of the audit committee's responsibilities. These should then be documented in an "Audit Committee Charter," to be included in the board bylaws. The charter effectively serves as the committee's road map, setting the direction for its actions, priorities, and boundaries. At a minimum, the charter should contain the qualifications for committee membership, define the committee's overall purpose, and describe its specific, recurring responsibilities. The charter also may describe the manner and frequency for communicating with the board of directors. To ensure that the committee's responsibilities meet the changing needs of the foundation, the full board should annually review and amend the charter as necessary.

Some foundations have no audit committee, while others have an audit committee functioning within the structure of the finance or investment committee. Although these approaches can work, they don't work well. They dilute the focus and limit the authority necessary for a well-functioning audit committee.

Committee Structure

The foundation's directors should select the audit committee members from among all directors, based on nominations made by the executive committee or the board chair. The nominating committee or committee on directors should continually keep audit committee responsibilities in mind as they develop a pipeline of foundations directors.

Three to five members constitute a reasonably sized audit committee. (An odd number prevents tie votes.) All members, including the chair, should be rotated off the committee at regular, staggered intervals to keep a fresh perspective, and the rotation process should be well planned so as to preserve the committee's institutional memory. When new members join the committee, there should be a formal process to ensure they understand their responsibilities and are prepared to spend the necessary time.

Audit committee members *must* possess financial knowledge — and at least one member should have significant financial expertise — but they also need a good deal of general business experience. Coupled with common sense, curiosity, and historical knowledge of the foundation, such experience enables audit committee members to ask relevant questions, evaluate responses, and make practical recommendations. More to the point, committee members with business acumen provide considerable value to the foundation not only in performing the committee's regular, recurring duties but also in dealing with difficult financial issues.

To provide the audit committee necessary autonomy to carry out its responsibilities, it generally should report directly to the executive committee or to the foundation board chair.

To be most effective, audit committees should meet at least three to four times each year. Two meetings are needed to review and consider the annual audit, and at least one other meeting is needed to address other concerns or important issues.

Committee Responsibilities

Although circumstances within a foundation will affect the audit committee's focus, there are specific, annually recurring responsibilities that all audit committees must address.

The committee selects and retains the independent accountant to audit the annual financial statements. One of the committee's most important duties is to hire independent accountants. The committee, not management, must have the authority to retain or, if necessary, replace the audit firm. Through their professional auditing services, the independent accountants satisfy a critical fiduciary obligation for all members of the board of directors. The audit committee, in its role as agent for the board of directors, is responsible for ensuring that the independent accountants satisfy this obligation. Thus, selecting a well-qualified, independent accountant is essential. The committee must take a leadership role in managing this important relationship.

In selecting an independent accountant, the committee should consider the size, industry experience, and reputation of the firm. Large national or international firms generally have deeper and broader industry experience, while local or regional firms may offer more stable personnel and personalized service.

Each year, generally after the annual audit is completed, the audit committee should evaluate the services performed by the independent accountant. Some foundations find it sensible to change accounting firms every five to seven years. While this practice may offer the benefits of a fresh perspective and help address concerns over competitive fees, it also has the disadvantage of disruption to management, and it can cause inefficiencies in the audit process. Periodically changing audit team staff and the audit partner without changing firms may be an acceptable alternative. Maintaining a cooperative, professional relationship with the firm is important, and a key element of that relationship is how the firm's representatives view the role of the committee. The audit firm should view the committee as its client.

The committee oversees the annual audit of the financial statements.

Ensuring that the annual financial statements are appropriately audited and that the Form 990 is accurate consumes the majority of the audit committee's time. This task usually requires multiple meetings, and the results of the process must be communicated to the full board. Generally, the oversight can be completed in two meetings, with one meeting occurring before the audit begins and the second occurring after the auditors have substantially completed their audit.

Before the audit begins, the committee should meet with the auditor to discuss the scope, process, and timing of the audit. Although management personnel also should attend this meeting, the audit committee has the prerogative to conduct parts of the meeting without management present. In discussing the scope of the audit, committee members should recognize that auditors are guided by certain professional standards in determining the audit's minimum scope and will exercise professional judgment in their approach.

The initial meeting also provides committee members a good opportunity to engage the auditor in discussions about specific areas of concern that may not be addressed in normal, recurring audit procedures. It may be cost prohibitive or impractical for the auditors to address each of the committee's concerns in one audit cycle, so the committee should arrange its concerns by priority. This way, the greatest concerns can be addressed quickly and others tackled in future audits. Auditors generally are not averse to expanding their procedures.

Because most auditors now employ a risk-based audit approach, their audit may not address all financial areas, or some areas may receive only limited attention. The committee should ask which areas the auditor considers high risk and which, if any, he or she plans to exclude based on a perceived low level of risk. It is as important to know the excluded areas as those areas to be included in the audit.

The committee also should ask whether the auditor plans to issue comments on internal control deficiencies noted during the audit or to report any opportunities for operational improvements. Generally, such comments are communicated in a document referred to as the "management letter." Such letters are common. They can be very helpful to the audit committee as well as management and should be encouraged.

It also is important for the committee to understand the auditor's general approach to evaluating internal controls as well as the specific approach to evaluating information technology controls. Rather than assuming that an evaluation of all controls, including information technology controls, will be included in the audit, committee members should inquire about the approach and extent of testing. Because of the critical importance of information technology in today's business world, it is a good practice to periodically review such controls as security over data and back-up and recovery procedures in the event of a natural disaster.

Finally, the audit committee should inquire about the type of audit report the auditor expects to issue on the financial statements. While the answer to this question will depend in part on the ensuing audit, the question nevertheless is timely. If it is possible or anticipated that the auditor's opinion may be "qualified" (that is, the auditor has discovered some problems along the way), the audit committee is obligated to notify the board chair as soon as possible. Qualified opinions reflect negatively on the foundation and the board, and donors and other important constituents will view them negatively as well. If the auditor anticipates issuing a qualified report, preventive actions may still be possible at this stage of the audit.

The committee reviews the work of the auditor. After the audit is substantially complete, the committee should meet with the auditor to review the financial statements and any findings and to ask relevant questions. This meeting should occur before the annual financial statements actually are issued, thus allowing time for any changes in format or content. Management should attend this meeting to review the financial statements and hear, firsthand, the auditor's findings. (The audit committee may choose to meet privately with the auditor later in the meeting; it generally is advisable to establish a pattern of routinely meeting privately with the auditor at the conclusion of each audit.)

Although the auditor is responsible for assessing the financial statements and reporting on the degree to which they present a fair picture of the financial condition of the foundation, the content of the financial statements are management's responsibility, and the audit committee should support management in this regard. The content and format of the financial statements must comply with "generally accepted accounting principles," though some flexibility is allowed. While the committee should seek the auditor's advice about any substantial changes to content or format, the committee should not allow the auditors to control the financial statements or the preparation process. Once the audit is complete, the auditors will issue their opinion on the financial statements.

At this meeting, the committee also should inquire about the status of the auditor's "management letter." This letter may describe weaknesses in the foundation's internal financial controls and include recommendations on operational improvements. The audit committee is responsible for ensuring that the letter's concerns are addressed. The committee may choose to review the letter during this meeting or defer the review until management responds to the letter. In either case, the disposition of the letter's contents should be documented and reported to the full board.

With the audit completed, the auditor can prepare Form 990. Alternatively, the foundation staff may prepare the form for the auditor's review. Before the form is filed with the Internal Revenue Service, the audit committee should review the document and address any concerns with the auditor or legal counsel, if necessary.

This meeting also offers a valuable opportunity for audit committee members to ask questions on a broad range of topics relating to the audit. These may include the following:

- Major audit issues;

- Difficulties in completing the audit;

- Management's responsiveness and overall level of cooperation;

- Alternative accounting principles to those used in the preparation of the financial statements;

- Number and size of auditor adjustments reflected in the financial statements;

- Number and type of audit adjustments not reflected in the financial statements;

- Management's overall approach to compliance with laws and regulations;

- The internal control system, including information technology controls; and

- Non-audit services performed by the auditor.

The audit committee must know of any non-audit services the independent auditor performs for the foundation or any related entities. Because non-audit services may damage or appear to jeopardize the auditor's objectivity in performing the audit services, committee members must know of these services and make their own determination of the effect or perceived effect on the auditor's independence. Indeed, the committee should have approval power over any non-audit services the firm may perform for the foundation. In general, hiring the auditor to consult on other financial or management matters should be the exception, not the rule.

108

Additional Audit Committee Functions

In addition to its annually recurring responsibilities, the audit committee can provide added value to management and assist the board of directors by addressing other areas of concern.

Maintaining integrity. Detecting and dealing with dishonesty is probably the most basic of audit functions. The foundation's internal control system must be designed to reduce temptation, deter dishonest actions, and detect any wrongdoing that occurs. While management is responsible for maintaining the internal control system, the audit committee is responsible for periodic oversight and high-level monitoring of the system.

Since cash is the asset most vulnerable to theft, cash-handling procedures, particularly at the point of entry to the system, should be designed to reduce opportunities for theft. Not only will this deter or prevent most thefts, it also is considerate to personnel because it avoids placing them in situations that test their honesty. The audit committee should inquire about the controls over cash and periodically request that auditors place additional emphasis on testing these controls. Standard audit procedures will include annual checks on fraud under SAS 99 audit regulations.

Ensuring experienced, trained, and competent staff. In many foundations, staff can turn over frequently. What's more, foundation work is heavily regulated, and the rules governing foundations' activities change frequently. Through input from the auditors, the audit committee can obtain an objective outsider's view on the capabilities of the foundation's management and financial staff. Also, if staff turnover appears excessive, the auditor may offer a perspective on the level of turnover compared with that of peer foundations or offer insights as to the nature of the turnover.

Although the audit committee must be sensitive to management's responsibility and authority over hiring, training, and retaining staff, the committee can work with management, encourage hiring plans that fill identified skills or capability gaps, and support continuing education programs.

Monitoring conflicts of interest. Audit committee members should completely understand the foundation's conflict-of-interest policy. Actual or perceived conflicts can damage a foundation's credibility; in extreme situations, conflicts may lead the IRS to revoke the foundation's tax-exempt status. The resulting loss in deductibility for donor contributions is the death penalty for a foundation.

109

Conflicts generally result from relationships — such as those with or between directors, employees, vendors, donors, and family members. Not surprisingly, potential conflicts commonly exist at foundations, and it is not the purpose of the conflict-of-interest policy to eliminate them. Instead, the policy should facilitate identification of potential conflicts and enable management and the board to consider them when conducting the foundation's business.

Committee members ordinarily should not have business relationships with the foundation or the related institution. When business relationships do exist, any conflicts of interest or the appearance of conflicts of interest should be documented and addressed. A simple question can guide the committee's consideration: How would this relationship affect our image if it were described in a newspaper?

The audit committee should determine that the conflict-of-interest policy adequately defines those relationships or situations that may give rise to conflicts. The audit committee should also oversee the annual reporting by board members in complying with the policy and assist executive management in addressing any potential conflicts.

Because of its critical role in ensuring the appropriate "tone" at the top of an organization, the audit committee also should encourage senior management to adopt a formal employee code of business conduct. The code should be a statement of the foundation's commitment to ethical behavior and set guidelines for acceptable and unacceptable behavior by staff and board members alike.

Monitoring travel and entertainment expense policies. Questionable or unauthorized "T&E" expenditures can embarrass and ultimately damage the foundation's image and reputation in the eyes of donors and other constituents.

The audit committee should determine that existing policies comply with IRS documentation requirements and that all expenditures are reviewed and approved by appropriate management personnel. When reviewing such policies, the audit committee should be alert to situations in which management personnel may be placed in the awkward position of reviewing or approving the T&E expenditures of their superiors.

Audit committee members possess a great wealth of business expertise. It should be expected, therefore, that foundation executives and board members will utilize this experience in addressing various foundation challenges. Although each foundation's unique circumstances and the inherent skills of the audit committee members will dictate when and how committee members will be called upon for assistance, some possible areas include incentive compensation plans, risk management, and information technology strategies.

As foundation boards address their constituents' demands for greater transparency and accountability, they logically will look closely at their governance structure and their own effectiveness. For the audit committee, this entails a periodic review of the effectiveness of individual members and that of the committee. The audit committee's charter can be an excellent yardstick for conducting periodic self-assessments.

The Development Committee

Royster C. Hedgepeth

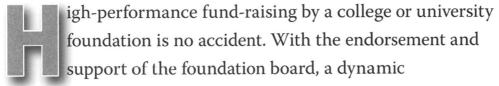igh-performance fund-raising by a college or university foundation is no accident. With the endorsement and support of the foundation board, a dynamic development committee can transform fund-raising from an annual struggle into a rewarding crusade. As a standing committee of the foundation's board of directors, the development committee provides the oversight needed for high-performance fund-raising, while it leads the involvement of the full board in the process.

The model presented in this chapter emphasizes a higher level of engagement and oversight by the development committee than typically has been the practice. The development committee's more assertive role as the board's agent leading the foundation's fund-raising efforts is grounded in four significant trends in philanthropy:

- An increasingly competitive fund-raising environment;

- Greater numbers of donors designating the use of their gifts and the resulting mandate for higher levels of performance accountability;

- Increasing engagement by donors, particularly younger philanthropists, in the implementation of programs initiated through their giving; and

- A reaffirmation of the critical role of volunteers as advocates for and partners in the philanthropic process.

Fund-raising today requires a new edge — a well-prepared development committee grounded in proven fundamentals and working in collaboration with foundation staff to produce significantly increased, sustainable fund-raising. A performance-based development committee has five readily identifiable characteristics:

1. Clearly defined expectations of the committee's fund-raising responsibilities and the fund-raising performance of its members;

2. Measurable outcomes that are evaluated on a regular basis for each set of responsibilities;

3. A powerful commitment to succeed, a clear understanding of what constitutes success, and a knowledge of what success means to the life of the institution;

4. A focused commitment to raising significant private dollars in support of the institution's mission, needs, and opportunities; and

5. Unwavering attention to sound fund-raising fundamentals, including an active program of donor stewardship that establishes the basis for future fund-raising efforts.

The sections that follow elaborate on each of these areas, provide illustrations and guidance on best practices, and give a sense of desired outcomes. The chapter includes both qualitative and quantitative guidelines for creating a performance-based development committee and performance-minded development committee members.

Clearly Defined Expectations

Not many of us would expect an athletic coach to put a team in game conditions without matching player skills to the position and providing thorough practice and preparation. Likewise, no one would expect a development committee to engage in high-performance fund-raising without well-defined expectations and proper education and skill development.

Members of the development committee should have a passion for their institution and its aspirations and should be willing to translate that passion into raising money. They should be people whose local, regional, national, or international knowledge allows them to foster philanthropic relationships. Most important, they must be able to set an example through their personal giving and engage the rest of the board in pacesetting giving. In addition to setting an example, committee members also create a philanthropic environment by opening doors to prospective donors, engaging and cultivating prospects, and actively soliciting gifts.

Members of the development committee also may be asked to assume additional responsibilities depending on the maturity of the foundation's fund-raising program. Some members will need to take responsibility for working with foundation staff to acquire major gifts — gifts valued at $100,000 to $1 million or more. Others will need to take the lead in identifying prospects and securing annual leadership gifts (those typically ranging from $1,000 to $25,000 per year).

If the foundation is responsible for the institution's broad-based annual fund, the committee also may engage volunteers who participate in direct-mail and telephone solicitation efforts.

The creation of a productive, performance-based development committee begins with a clear statement of the committee's purposes that expresses how fulfillment of those purposes will benefit the foundation and the institution. The statement should include a concise job description for committee members that establishes performance expectations and the process of evaluating performance.

The development committee's volunteer structure should be led by board members, but the membership of these subgroups need not be limited to board members. Such involvement offers an important training ground for future board membership.

Years ago, during the national phase of the Campaign for the University of Illinois, foundation staff developed a concise handbook that was used to enlist and prepare campaign volunteers. It included a timeline that specified when education and preparation would be provided and when each volunteer's participation was needed. Your development committee might develop a similar guide that might include the following:

Background

- Brief history and status of the fund-raising program;

- Foundation fund-raising goals and their linkage to the institution's mission, needs, and opportunities;

- Timetable for education, skills development, and program implementation;

- Sample of research about prospects and opportunities for giving; and

- Overview of the fund-raising process and upcoming training opportunities.

Committee Purposes and Goals

- Raise philanthropic support that improves the quality of education for students;

- Strengthen the foundation's reputation and the institution's image;

- Enlist additional volunteers who can contribute to increased fund-raising action; and

- Set the foundation board's standards for gift-giving and gift-getting.

Individual Committee Member Responsibilities

+ Set an example with individual committee member giving;

+ Set the standard for understanding the institution's needs and opportunities for private support;

+ Know, understand, and participate in the fund-raising cycle; and

+ Be accountable for fund-raising performance.

Regardless of the expectations, performance-based development committee action is not serendipitous. Successful committees require careful selection and assignment, thorough planning, disciplined implementation, and an uncommon commitment by foundation staff, board leaders, and committee members. Although the staff is responsible for guiding and supporting the committee's planning, preparation, and action, the committee must ensure that that the staff has been given clear performance expectations and evaluations, an appropriate budget, and the volunteer commitment they need to be successful.

Measurable Outcomes and Regular Evaluation

Perhaps the single most difficult barrier to creating a performance-based development committee is resistance to regular performance evaluations of both the committee as a group and of individual committee members. During the selection, assignment, and preparation stages of the committee's work, clear expectations must be established. The committee should select a limited number of measurable outcomes to which the committee and its members will be committed.

First, a development committee should set expectations for the amount of money it expects to raise. The anticipated tactical approaches and the collaborative responsibilities of the staff and volunteers will help determine these expectations. Interim objectives should be set for progress on both dollar goals and the activities that produce successful fund-raising.

Second, the committee should set expectations for the use of the money that is being raised. The committee should examine regularly how well its efforts produce results that address the institution's aspirations for service, growth, and development.

Third, the development committee should set philanthropic expectations for all foundation board members and regularly assess their performance relative to those expectations. The committee should make clear to all board members that they are expected to (1) make meaningful gifts proportional to both the campaign goal and their individual financial capacity and (2) identify, cultivate, and solicit other prospects as needed.

The committee's assessment of its performance as a corporate body should do four things:

- Establish benchmarks for future efforts;

- Provide accountability for current efforts;

- Inform the future direction and structure of the committee's efforts; and

- Set the tone for the full board's commitment to fund-raising.

A Powerful Commitment to Success

The development committee makes certain that fund-raising priorities and productivity are never taken for granted. One of the most fascinating fund-raising meetings in my experience occurred when a development committee strenuously challenged its foundation's executive staff to announce a goal that was 25 percent larger than its original proposal. The committee's aspirations carried the day, and its commitment to success kept everyone focused on performance. As a result, the larger goal was surpassed dramatically — and ahead of time.

The development committee demonstrates its commitment to success by asking difficult questions about fund-raising. The following three sets of questions may be helpful. The first set is qualitative, the second set more quantitative in nature, and the third set is procedural.

Qualitative questions

1. Does the foundation have a focused, exciting case that supports the institution's mission and aspirations?

2. Has the development committee created a steady flow of new prospective donors and an assertive program of engaging them in the life of the institution?

3. Is philanthropy a part of the daily life and culture of the foundation board and the institution? Is the difference philanthropy is making in the quality of the institution and the life of its community visible to the outside observer?

4. Are there effective partnerships between and among the development committee, the foundation board, the foundation staff, the institution's president and executive leadership, and the institutional governing board?

5. Is the development committee "leading by example"? Is the board following?

6. Does the foundation's program of accountability and stewardship actively engage donors and prepare the way for future fund-raising?

Quantitative questions

1. Has the development committee defined goals for fund-raising and a timetable to accomplish them? Is responsibility for their accomplishment clearly assigned?

2. In conjunction with foundation staff, has the committee set performance goals for each of the components of the fund-raising program?

3. Does the development committee have clear performance guidelines and a schedule of assessment for the committee as a whole and for its individual members?

4. Does the foundation board — led by the development committee — have fund-raising goals for which the entire board is responsible? Are those performance goals assessed on a regular basis?

5. Is the board's leadership in terms of giving assessed and reported regularly?

Procedural questions

1.   Does the foundation have a specific plan for selecting, preparing, and assessing members of the development committee?

2. Do development committee members have specific assignments and expectations of performance?

3. Does the committee have a schedule for major-gift solicitations of the size and scope needed for success?

4. Does the committee have a formal gift-acceptance policy? Is it adhered to and reviewed on a regular basis?

5. Does the committee effectively account for fund-raising results and engage donors through an active stewardship program?

Focused Commitment to Raising Significant Private Dollars

Foundations can raise money for just about anything, but not for *everything*. Thus, the first measure of an effective foundation development committee is its ability to maintain a clear sense of the purposes for which it is raising money and how those resources support the college or university's priorities.

Our colleges and universities want to attract students and faculty, provide the best laboratories and equipment, and strengthen the environment in which teaching and learning take place. Ultimately, college and university foundations want to make a difference in the lives of students and, through them, improve the quality of life for all of us. To do this, the institutions they serve need scholarships, professorships, research funds, equipment, buildings, and various other tangible items that contribute to excellence.

117

Each of these has a price tag, so it's easy to lose track of the real value of fund-raising as we answer the question, "How much did we raise?" The development committee has a special mandate to see that institutions, donors, and beneficiaries never lose track of the value of philanthropy. After all, donors don't make gifts because institutions need the money. They give because they want good things to happen for students and faculty.

At the same time, no one should underestimate the importance of the amount of money being raised. Year-to-year and peer comparisons can offer significant insights into whether a committee really is succeeding at raising money. Many college and university foundation boards were spoiled in the 1980s and 1990s by the unbroken, upward slope of fund-raising results. They thought annual increases of up to 20 percent were a sure thing. This expectation encountered a severe reality check in 2001 and 2002. Today's development committee needs to understand natural fluctuations in the market, keep close tabs on the dollar value of funds being raised, and be responsive to changing philanthropic patterns.

As the pressure increases on foundations to raise unrestricted dollars to offset decreasing state revenues, the development committee needs to provide a careful accounting of funds received based on the source, type, and size of gifts. Multiyear performance analysis can identify trends and enable the committee to work with the institution to set challenging yet achievable goals and to incorporate philanthropy more effectively into the overall resource model — keeping in mind that the trend toward donor designation of gifts does not support the desire for numerous or large unrestricted gifts.

The development committee also needs to recognize and monitor the activities that contribute to raising money successfully. These measures include the following:

- The total number of prospects being actively cultivated, solicited, and stewarded;

- The number of development activities staff are taking in a disciplined fashion;

- The value of solicitations outstanding and pledges payable;

- The number of new prospects being identified and incorporated in the process; and

- The level of activity in which development committee and other board members are involved.

Effective fund-raising is an intense, complex business. In overseeing the success of the foundation's fund-raising efforts, the development committee needs to exhibit a high level of sophistication about raising money and creating a philanthropic environment that fosters success.

Unwavering Attention to Fund-Raising Fundamentals

Among top-performing foundation boards, virtually all directors are involved in fund-raising activities. They demonstrate their leadership by identifying prospective donors, assisting in the cultivation and solicitation of those donors, and maintaining the highest standards of accountability regarding the donor's gift. But there are no magic incantations that guarantee sustained fund-raising performance. Rather, the development committee can achieve the highest levels of fund-raising performance by doing the following:

- Consciously and intentionally engaging and assessing the participation of board members based on the ways in which they can be most effective;

- Creating expectations for top performance, establishing standards of performance in each fund-raising component, and ensuring maximum productivity and sustainability; and

- Applying rigorous timetables and measurement to motivate and support the foundation's fund-raising efforts.

While the business of fund-raising is complex, its conceptual framework is quite simple. The framework starts with an understanding of the priorities for fund-raising, the value being added, and the fund-raising game plan endorsed by the foundation board. The charge to the development committee should be rooted in the definition of the committee's responsibilities articulated in the foundation's bylaws. For example, the bylaws might state the following:

> *The development committee of the board of directors is responsible for the foundation's comprehensive fund-raising program. In carrying out its duties, the committee will set clear expectations and timetables for all phases of fund-raising activity and report the results of those efforts to the full board on a quarterly basis. The committee will be chaired by a member of the board of directors and include at least X members of the board. Up to Y additional members may be added to the committee or its subcommittees. The development committee works in concert with the foundation's executive staff and the university's executive leadership to determine fund-raising goals, priorities, and timetables.*

The fund-raising cycle, properly maintained, reinvents itself continually, as the figure on page 120 demonstrates.

Within the fund-raising process, opportunities exist for every director to contribute to fund-raising success in meaningful ways. The development committee is responsible for seeing that each director's participation is compatible with his or her interests and capabilities, that staff provides effective preparation for and coordination of all board-related fund-raising activity, and that superior performance is expected, recognized, and rewarded.

Setting Priorities. The development committee is responsible for seeing that effective decisions are made about the priorities for fund-raising. Those priorities should be set in support of the institution's most compelling needs and opportunities.

Effective fund-raising priorities assure prospective donors that their gifts will be meaningful and will make a positive difference in creating the future of the college or university. Well-selected priorities also provide the forces needed for mobilizing the development committee's fund-raising efforts. Setting priorities that are integral to the institution's future also contributes to the sense of energy and urgency that drives successful fund-raising. Sound fund-raising plans based on high-value priorities facilitate the development committee's efforts in each phase of the fund-raising process.

Establish Fund-Raising Plans and Priorities

Steward the Results of Gifts Received

Identify and Qualify Prospective Donors

Follow-Through/Close Gift Commitments

Cultivate/Engage Prospective Donors

Ask for the Investment

THE FUND-RAISING CYCLE

Identification and Qualification. Qualified prospective donors are the essential ingredient of successful fund-raising. The reality is that gifts come from individuals, corporations, and foundations that have either a special relationship with the institution or a vested interest in its success. The development committee should make certain that committee members, other foundation directors, and carefully selected volunteers continuously identify new prospective donors and help create new relationships.

For many development committees, the ongoing identification and qualification of new prospective donors is cyclical; it hits a high point in preparation for a formal campaign and often lies fallow the rest of the time. For top-performing development committees, donor identification and qualification is a way of life. Each quarter the development committee should assess its progress in terms of the following:

• The number of new major-gift and leadership-gift prospects identified through the committee's efforts,

- The number of prospects whose status has been upgraded as a result of the committee's efforts,

- The effectiveness of the information provided about prospects (whether the identification and qualification process led to a gift or to involvement in activities that lead to solicitation and giving),

- The percentage of board members actively involved in the process, and

- The schedule for sustaining identification and qualifying activity.

Cultivation. Cultivation incorporates the various strategies used to involve prospective donors in the institution's life. Those who take part in the university's programs and initiatives are more likely to make larger philanthropic commitments than those who are not. They experience firsthand the potential their philanthropy creates; they know how and why their gifts will have an impact.

121

Identifying opportunities to involve donors and prospective donors is one of the most important contributions the development committee can elicit from its fellow board members. Under committee guidance, directors can accompany prospects to artistic, cultural, educational, and athletic events. They can arrange meals with the university president or key university leaders. They can listen to prospective donors to learn what interests might spark a philanthropic link to the institution. Board and committee members also can make suggestions about specific areas of service or involvement that may be especially meaningful to the prospect.

The keys to success for the development committee's cultivation efforts are paying regular, disciplined attention to the donor and ensuring that the donor perceives the university as part of his or her life. The development committee should establish the expectation that all directors will find ways to help ensure the university's place in the hearts and minds of potential donors. It should also help ensure that directors experience success in these efforts.

To measure success in this regard, the development committee should regularly assess the following:

- The scope, volume, and regularity of cultivation activities that engage prospective donors in the life of the institution;

- The number of prospective donors being prepared for solicitation and their progress through the cultivation cycle leading to solicitation; and

• The degree to which leadership-giving and donor-stewardship activities are integrated into the program of prospect cultivation.

Asking. Many people choose to make a significant philanthropic investment in a university simply because they are asked to do so. In every successful fund-raising effort, a small group of volunteers, usually development committee members and board officers, will become significantly involved in gift solicitation. Although no single personality type or outward style defines the successful solicitor, the development committee should educate all board members about the basics of successful solicitation. Then, when the opportunity presents itself, each director will be ready to perform effectively.

The top-performing development committee sees that successful solicitors are well prepared. The development committee's efforts make certain that solicitors are aware of the institution's needs, opportunities, and aspirations. Well-prepared solicitors can articulate the case for support, and they are familiar with the concerns of those they are going to solicit. Successful solicitors also understand the value of the gifts for which they are asking and where such gifts fit in the institution's philanthropic plans.

Good solicitors rarely act alone. They communicate and collaborate with one another and the foundation's professional staff to increase their chance for success, and they engage other board members and key volunteers to strengthen their case and provide powerful personal endorsements. Members of the development committee should set the example for all volunteer solicitors in their practice of these principles. In addition, the committee can monitor the following indicators:

• The value of outstanding solicitations; solicitations planned within 30, 60, or 90 days; requests affirmed and denied in the prior 30 days;

• Whether the value of solicitation activity is sufficient to meet established goals;

• The percentage of ongoing solicitation activity that involves committee and board members as primary participants; and

• The extent to which communication and coordination of solicitation efforts are being led and monitored by the foundation's executive staff.

Follow-Through and Closing. Once a solicitation has been made, a prospective donor may want additional information, an opportunity to discuss the proposal with a spouse or financial adviser, or a chance to attend to various other matters that may defer a decision. Development committee members, key volunteers, and foundation staff should stay in close communication with the prospect during this period of negotiation. Together, they can provide additional information and foster ongoing engagement.

Effective closing may involve a second or third solicitation as new information comes to light and the prospect goes through the decision-making process. After the prospect agrees to make a gift, the development committee member and foundation professional work together to formalize arrangements. The process for confirming gift commitments should be established by the development committee.

The committee can monitor the following:

- Whether the committee has a process to monitor outstanding requests, seek committee or board input and participation, and ensure ongoing contact with the prospect once the ask has been made;

- Whether the level of committee and board participation is sufficient to maximize the opportunity for success; and

- Whether the ratio of requests to gifts made fits within the organization's proposed gift tables and indicates effective fund-raising performance.

Stewardship. Stewardship of gifts a donor already has made is the most powerful form of cultivation. In engaging the donor about the difference his or her gift has made and in involving the donor in the results, the development committee most clearly establishes the institution's position to ask for additional, larger gifts. The development committee supports every donor's right to know that a gift has been used as it was intended, that the gift made a difference, and what that difference was.

Foundation staff members are responsible for most of the communication with donors, acknowledging receipt of their gifts, thanking them for their support, and telling them of the important value added through their generosity. Many foundation executives go to great lengths to connect students who received scholarships funded through gifts with their donors. Several foundations have scholarship recognition dinners at which donors ceremonially present their scholarship awards to the recipients. The relationships established and the vitality created transcend the dollar value of any gift and often lead to additional and larger gifts.

The development committee should ensure that these donor-relations functions are discharged fully and effectively. In many cases, committee members can take a personal role in affirming the practical value of a donor's gift, thus helping set the stage for future requests. A few indicators the committee can monitor include the following:

- Whether a written plan for donor stewardship exists;

- Whether a process exists to keep donors informed and involved in the benefits their philanthropy is making possible; and

- Whether donors express satisfaction that their gifts are being used as they expected and are having the desired impact.

Gift-Acceptance Policy. Adoption of an effective gift-acceptance policy is one of the cornerstones of the development committee's oversight of stewardship to donors. The foundation's policy should state how and for what purposes gifts of cash, securities, and personal property will be accepted. By and large, these are straightforward procedures. Four types of gifts require particular attention:

1. **Restricted gifts.** The foundation's gift-acceptance policy should define the framework within which donors may designate the use of their gifts and limitations on such specificity. If a gift is overly restrictive or is not in keeping with the institution's mission, the gift-acceptance policy provides the foundation and the institution with the ability to reject it or to suggest alternatives. Some gifts may raise potential liabilities, especially if a prospective donor wishes to shape institutional direction through restrictions on the gift and inappropriate personal involvement with the organization. While the practice of placing restrictions on gifts is not new, an effective gift-acceptance policy creates a framework for determining the nature and extent of acceptable designations.

2. **Gifts of real estate.** These gifts offer the donor and the institution mutually beneficial opportunities for philanthropic investment. The foundation, however, is responsible for seeing that due diligence is exercised before a gift of real estate is accepted. The foundation's consideration must include, but is not limited to, environmental risk and impact assessments, evaluation of financial obligations and risks, and potential tax or other legal liabilities.

3. **Gifts of personal property.** The foundation's gift-acceptance policy also should provide specific provisions governing the acceptance and valuation of gifts of personal property, especially gifts of art. The foundation should be certain that gifts of personal property fit the institutional mission or can be converted to provide resources that do so. The Internal Revenue Service has specific guidelines for such gifts.

4. **Gifts of technology and intellectual property.** Such gifts also require special attention. Examining whether a gift fits with the institution's mission and establishing a gift's valuation for reporting purposes are two of the issues that need to be addressed.

A well-conceived gift-acceptance policy created by the development committee and endorsed by the foundation board establishes a framework of trust and respect that undergirds good donor relations throughout the philanthropic process. AGB provides an illustrative gift-acceptance policy (see Appendix E).

Accounting and Accountability. Most foundations do an excellent job of receiving gifts, providing a tax receipt to donors, and accounting for gift activity on a regular basis. In addition to providing accurate gift totals, gift reports to the foundation board should provide details on the source and the use of gifts by category. These definitions provide an important step in the stewardship process as they link philanthropy to the institutional mission and its supporters. The stewardship process, in turn, provides important opportunities for foundation board members to participate meaningfully in the fund-raising process.

In like manner, the foundation board's aggregate giving should be reviewed on a regular basis by the development committee and, through the committee, by the board. The review of board giving should provide an accurate record of directors' participation in annual, capital, and deferred giving. Each year, the executive committee (or the committee on directors) should review the giving records of individual board members as part of the annual board and director performance review. This review compares actual results against expectations for board leadership in philanthropic giving.

While the finance or audit committee usually is responsible for the foundation's financial audit and meeting the technical requirements of gift giving and receiving, the development committee should ensure that personal conversations take place with *all* donors to let them know that their gifts make a difference. In monitoring their responsibilities for regular, ongoing communication of both audit compliance (accounting) and stewardship (the value that has been added by private giving), the development committee should examine the following:

- Whether the development committee communicates the results of the foundation's audit to donors and other stakeholders on a timely basis;

- Whether the committee's oversight of effective donor communication is exercised in a timely fashion; and

- Whether the committee's program of donor stewardship is personal, engaging, and continuous.

Coordination and Communication. Successful fund-raising is a team effort. While development committee members must always be alert to a "philanthropic moment" on behalf of the university, they also should be aware of the need to coordinate with the foundation's professional staff. Development committee members should expect the professional staff to do the following:

- Work with directors to identify and select appropriate prospective donors;

- Provide the skills development and preparation necessary for success;

- Prepare the background information necessary for effective solicitation;

- Develop the case for support and any related materials;

- Follow through promptly on requests for additional information or support; and

- Acknowledge and recognize directors' efforts.

Similarly, the foundation's fund-raising staff should expect the development committee, its members, and other volunteer fund-raisers to do the following:

- Understand the fund-raising process and the multiple roles important to success;

- Prepare themselves thoroughly for their role as volunteer fund-raisers;

- Make their own gift in proportion to the gifts for which they are asking;

- Complete assignments as expeditiously as possible;

- Submit appropriate reports in a timely fashion;

- Operate as a member of the team and communicate regularly on all fund-raising activities and assignments; and

- See that fund-raising is a foundation board priority and involve other directors at every opportunity.

An effective foundation staff provides the plan, framework, and support that are essential to the success of their volunteers. Good development committee members provide an authentication for the university's fund-raising efforts that cannot be found elsewhere.

Conclusion

The development committee's role in high-performance fund-raising is both intense and assertive. At the same time, the committee cannot substitute for or micromanage the foundation staff in planning, implementing, and monitoring the fund-raising process. Effective foundation development committees are partners in creating and supporting productive, comprehensive fund-raising programs for their colleges and universities.

In today's highly competitive, constantly evolving fund-raising environment, creating and maintaining a performance-based foundation board development committee is an essential ingredient of philanthropic success. A top-performing development committee combines the best of strategy, structure, and systems with the positive dynamic of human-relations skills to create a vital, productive program. In the process, the development committee stresses planning and priorities, creates focus and a sense of urgency, leads by example, prepares volunteers and assesses and rewards their performance, demands accountability, celebrates success, and sustains continuity.

Margin of Excellence
THE NEW WORK OF HIGHER EDUCATION FOUNDATIONS

APPENDICES

APPENDIX A

Responsibilities of Foundation Boards

- Approve (and periodically review) the foundation's statement of mission and purposes

- Promote strong and healthy relationships between the foundation and its host institution, and between the public and the foundation

- Appoint and support *the foundation chief executive* (the appointment process may be a responsibility shared with others)

131

- Monitor and assess the performance of *the foundation chief executive* (may also be a shared responsibility)

- Periodically and comprehensively assess *the board's performance,* preferably with competent third party help (ideally every three to four years)

- Regularly review the performance of *individual board members* who are eligible for renewal of their terms

- Ensure that all fiduciary responsibilities are met, including effective management of assets

- Insist on good planning for the foundation, consistent and complementary with the host institution's plan and priorities

- Ensure adequate resources through active fund-raising, asset management, and advocacy programs

- Protect donor rights and honor gift instructions

APPENDIX B

Responsibilities of Foundation Board Members

- Articulate and support *the foundation's* mission, purpose, and responsibilities

- Understand and support *the host institution's* mission, goals, and priorities

- Understand your fiduciary responsibilities

- Prepare for and participate conscientiously in board and committee meetings and other foundation activities

- Ask good questions and willingly share time and expertise

- Actively participate in the fund-raising process:

  - Set an example through personal giving (annual giving and periodic campaigns)

  - Encourage donor participation and ensure donor confidence

  - Identify and cultivate prospects (help open doors)

  - Solicit gifts

  - Encourage that gifts and donors be properly acknowledged

- Advocate for the foundation and the host institution at every opportunity

- Scrupulously avoid even the appearance of conflict of interest and adhere to foundation policy

- Be alert to prospective and influential candidates to fill vacancies on the board (always with care and through the appropriate board committee)

APPENDIX C
Memorandum of Understanding
Between a Foundation and Host Institution or System

Preamble

Public college and university foundations are incorporated 501 (c) (3) organizations affiliated with two-year or four-year publicly supported postsecondary institutions.

Foundations exist to raise and manage private resources supporting the mission and priorities of public institutions, and provide opportunities for students and a margin of institutional excellence unavailable with state funds.

The basic foundation structure tends to be fairly consistent across higher education, although variations exist based on institutional setting (some foundations are related to a single campus, others to a system that has separate campus-based foundations) and the degree of foundation independence (fully dependent on institutional support; interdependent, with partial support emanating from the related institution; or fully independent or autonomous). Foundation responsibilities, operations, and funding vary from state to state and institution to institution. A foundation may support a single campus or an entire system. Individual institutions within a system may have separate foundations as may individual schools or divisions within an institution.

Working with a national task force, the Association of Governing Boards of Universities and Colleges (AGB) and the Council for Advancement and Support of Education (CASE), have jointly developed an illustrative Memorandum of Understanding (MOU) for institutions and foundations. It is presented for consideration at a time when many public institutions and foundations are reviewing or redrafting their current working agreements. It is not intended to serve as a formal document recommended for adoption by all institutions or systems and their related foundations. Rather, the illustrative MOU is designed to enumerate elements that "best practice" suggests need to be considered for inclusion. History, campus culture, and legal dictates ultimately will affect the contents of particular MOUs.

In some states foundation status is determined by state legislation. State court rulings have established various interpretations of foundation independence. Institution and foundation counsel should be consulted in all instances where the MOU (the legal contract that defines the working relationship between an institution or system and its related foundation) is being reviewed. Special attention should be paid to governance, use of state funds, staffing, and other issues that have a significant bearing on foundation independence.

The MOU should not be lengthy, but it should include the following elements:

- An introduction that summarizes the overall relationships between the foundation and its host institution or system. This statement should broadly define the foundation's responsibilities and clarify the foundation's standing as an independent public trust. The introduction should provide the foundation with the appropriate authority to use its own name and service marks and the name and service marks of the institution in the conduct of its work. It should specify that the assets the foundation holds are dedicated to support the mission of the host institution or system.

- A description of the governance and leadership selection process of the institution or system and the foundation.

- An outline of the responsibilities and mutual expectations of the institution or system and the foundation.

- A statement on foundation and institution or system accountability.

- A brief overview on how funds shall be transferred between the foundation and the institution or system.

- A description of donor and alumni records owned either by the institution or foundation and policies governing the use and sharing of such records.

- A description of foundation administrative structure and how the foundation is financed.

- Definitions of terms and conditions, including circumstances for terminating the relationship or the dissolution of the foundation and distribution of the assets it holds.

- A formal adoption of the MOU by the institution's and/or system governing board's leaders and the foundation board's leadership.

Not all MOUs will contain each of these elements; however, to facilitate a favorable and productive relationship between the two parties, the agreement should at least consider these issues for inclusion. MOUs should demonstrate to the many constituencies of a public higher education institution or system that a formal set of understandings exists with the related foundation. In today's litigious society, a clearly articulated MOU is a useful instrument in establishing and reinforcing the foundation's legal standing.

AGB and CASE recognize that despite similar responsibilities and structures, foundations and institutions have nuanced missions and relationships, with special issues that require careful consideration.

These two are especially important:

- **Institution–Foundation Relationship**

  The MOU should clearly define the relationship between the institution or system and the foundation. A fully autonomous or independent foundation should clearly articulate its relationship with the host institution. An interdependent foundation should clearly articulate its standing as a separate 501(c)(3) organization serving a public trust; such a statement may help protect the foundation's donor-privacy policy from challenging litigation. In crafting the MOU, foundation officials should pay close attention to those areas that they consider important to remain confidential.

- **Compensation of the Institution or System Chief Executive and Other Senior University Administrative Staff**

  While it is fairly common practice for a foundation to supplement the compensation of an institution or system chief executive (and other senior university administrative staff), AGB and CASE encourage governing boards to assume full responsibility for providing for the compensation of institutional leaders. When private support is necessary, institutions and foundations should structure such supplements in ways that limit the foundation's influence in presidential selection or oversight.

  AGB and CASE commend this illustrative Memorandum of Understanding to their members for consideration when drafting or revising their own such documents. Both organizations welcome reactions and suggested improvements to the document.

Task Force

James Lanier *(chair)* emeritus president, East Carolina University Foundation

David Bahlmann, president and chief executive officer, Ball State University Foundation

Brad Barber, assistant vice president for institutional advancement, University of California System

Roger Blunt, chair, University of Maryland Foundation and president and chief executive officer, Blunt Enterprises, LLC

Louis Friedrich, former board chair, University of Illinois Foundation and managing director, Bernstein Investment Research and Management

Richard Imwalle, president and chief executive officer, University of Arizona Foundation

Richard Legon, executive vice president, AGB

Hon. Diana Murphy, chair, University of Minnesota Foundation; Board of Directors, AGB; U.S. Circuit Judge for the U.S. Court of Appeals for the Eighth Circuit

Robert T. Tad Perry, executive director, South Dakota Board of Regents

Gary A. Ransdell, president, Western Kentucky University

Thomas A. Roha, partner, Roha & Flaherty

Charles Steger, president, Virginia Tech

AGB/CASE Staff

Doreen Knapp Riley, director, foundation programs, AGB

David Bass, director, National Center for Affiliated Foundations, CASE

AGB-CASE Illustrative Memorandum of Understanding

Between a Foundation and Host Institution or System

NOTE: AGB and CASE commend this illustrative Memorandum of Understanding to their members for consideration when drafting or revising their own such documents. The following illustrative document includes examples of best practice that each foundation and host institution or system should consider based upon their own needs and relationship. Foundations and institutions are encouraged to consult with legal counsel when developing an MOU to ensure that the final document conforms with federal and state laws and policies. Please contact AGB or CASE to receive a current version of this illustrative MOU including comments on its content and application.

THIS AGREEMENT, entered into as of this _____ day of _____, 200___, by and between the _____ and the _____ .

The foundation was organized and incorporated in _____ for the purpose of stimulating voluntary private support from alumni, parents, friends, corporations, foundations, and others for the benefit of _____.

The _____ exists to raise and manage private resources supporting the mission and priorities of the _____, and provide opportunities for students and a margin of institutional excellence unavailable with state funds.

The foundation is dedicated to assisting the university in the building of the endowment and in addressing, through financial support, the long-term academic and other priorities of the university. *[Note: The MOU should reflect the specific responsibilities assumed by the foundation in addition to or in lieu of fund-raising responsibilities].*

As stated in its articles of incorporation, the foundation is a separately incorporated 501 (c) (3) organization and is responsible for identifying and nurturing relationships with potential donors and other friends of the _____ _____ ; soliciting cash, securities, real and intellectual property, and other private resources for the support of the _____ ; and acknowledging and stewarding such gifts in accordance with donor intent and its fiduciary responsibilities.

Furthermore, in connection with its fund-raising and asset-management activities, the foundation retains personnel experienced in planning for and managing private contributions and works with the university to assist and advise in such activities. [Note: Not all foundations retain personnel; in such instances personnel conducting foundation business report to other institutional staff].

In consideration of the mutual commitments herein contained, and other good and valuable consideration, receipt of which is hereby acknowledged, the parties agree as follows:

Foundation Name, Seal, and Logotype

Consistent with its mission to help to advance the plans and objectives of the university, the foundation is granted the use of the name, _____; however, the foundation will operate under its own seal and logotype and shall not use the university seal or other identifying marks in the promotion of its business and activities. *[Note: It is not unusual for foundations, upon mutual agreement, to have the authority to use the institution's seal and marks].*

Institution or System Governance

The _____ of the _____ is responsible for overseeing the mission, leadership, and operations of the university.

The _____ is responsible for setting priorities and long-term plans for the _____.

The _____ is legally responsible for the performance and oversight of all aspects of _____ [operations.

The _____ is responsible for the employment, compensation, and evaluation of all _____ employees, including the president [or chancellor].

The Foundation's Relationship to the Institution

- The _____ is a separately incorporated 501 (c) (3) non-profit organization created to raise, manage, distribute, and steward private resources to support the various missions of the university. *[Note: Language should be added to clarify the exact entity the foundation supports — e.g., a systemwide university, a single campus, an academic unit within university, or a campus within system.]*

- The_____ board of directors is responsible for the control and management of all assets of the foundation, including the prudent management of all gifts consistent with donor intent.

141

- The_____ is responsible for the performance and oversight of all aspects of its operations based on a comprehensive set of bylaws that clearly address the board's fiduciary responsibilities, including expectations of individual board members based upon ethical guidelines and policies.

- The_____ is responsible for the employment, compensation, and evaluation of all its employees, including the foundation chief executive. *[Note: MOU language should clarify whether the foundation has its own employees or relies on university employees to fulfill its responsibilities.]*

- The _____ may earmark a portion of its unrestricted funds to a discretionary fund for the president or chancellor of the university and will either transfer a percentage of those funds annually to the institution in compliance with state law and university policies or reimburse appropriate presidential expenditures. *[Note: All such expenditures must comply with the I.R.S. 501 (c) (3) code and be consistent with the foundation's mission. Such funds will be audited as part of the foundation's annual independent audit].*

The Institution's Relationship to the Foundation

- The university _____ is responsible for communicating _____ priorities and long-term plans, as approved by the board, to the foundation.

- The _____recognizes that the foundation is a private corporation with the authority to keep all records and data confidential consistent with the law.

- The chief executive of the foundation shall be included as a member of the university chief executive's cabinet and senior administrative team. *[Note: If the foundation is totally independent, the chief executive should have regular access to this group, and language in this document should reflect this.]*

- The _____ shall include the foundation as an active and prominent participant in the strategic planning for the university.

- The president or chancellor of the university shall serve as an ex officio member of the foundation board and shall assume a prominent role in fund-raising activities. *[Note: This can be with or without vote. Consult legal counsel for the most appropriate structure, and factor that into the language.]*

- In consideration for foundation services including but not limited to the _____ will provide the foundation with fair and reasonable compensation or payment for services. The amount of compensation will be negotiated on an annual basis by _____ of the preceding year. In consideration of foundation services, the _____ will also provide in-kind support including _____. *[Note: Institution support for foundation services may be detailed in a separate contract for services. Also, if the foundation does not receive any funding from the institution or system, then language should specify this.]*

- The _____ shall establish and enforce policies that support the _____ 's ability to respect the privacy and confidentiality of donor records.

Foundation Responsibilities

Fund-Raising

- The_____ shall create an environment conducive to increasing levels of private support for the mission and priorities of the _____ _____.

- The _____ , in consultation with the university _____ , is responsible for planning and executing comprehensive fund-raising and donor-acquisition programs in support of the institution's mission. These programs include annual giving, major gifts, planned gifts, special projects, and campaigns as appropriate. *[Note: When there are shared responsibilities for fund-raising, or if the university is responsible for all fund-raising activities, language should be added that clarifies each entity's roles and responsibilities. For example: The university desires to hire the expertise of the foundation to provide coordination and assistance in the operation, development, accounting, management, and marketing activities of the university development office. Or: The foundation desires to provide such services, not as an employee or agent of the university, but as an independent organization.]*

- The_____ will establish, adhere to, and periodically assess its gift-management and acceptance policies. It will promptly acknowledge and issue receipts for all gifts on behalf of the foundation and the university and provide appropriate recognition and stewardship of such gifts.

- The_____ recognizes that the foundation bears major responsibility for fund-raising. University representatives will coordinate fund-raising initiatives including major gifts solicitations with the foundation.

- The university will work in conjunction with the leadership of the foundation board and the foundation chief executive to identify, cultivate, and solicit prospects for private gifts.

- The_____ shall not accept grants from state or federal agencies, except in special circumstances that are approved by the foundation board of directors and the governmental agency. [Note: Some foundations, such as those serving in support of university health centers, can be called upon to accept and manage governmental grants].

- The_____ shall establish and enforce policies to protect donor confidentiality and rights.

Asset Management

- The _____will establish asset-allocation, disbursement, and spending policies that adhere to applicable federal and state laws including the Uniform Prudent Investor Act (UPIA) and the Uniform Management of Institutional Funds Act (UMIFA).

143

- The _____ will receive, hold, manage, invest, and disperse contributions of cash, securities, patents, copyrights, and other forms of property, including immediately vesting gifts and deferred gifts that are contributed in the form of planned and deferred-gift instruments.

- The _____ will engage an independent accounting firm annually to conduct an audit of the foundation's financial and operational records and will provide the _____ with a copy of the annual audited financial statements, including management letters. *[Note: Management letters, designed to affect management procedures, are typically shared with institutional presidents or chancellors in those cases where the foundation is dependent or interdependent].*

144

Institutional Flexibility

- The_____ will explore current opportunities, including acquisition and management of real estate on behalf of the _____ for future allocation, transfer, or use.

- The_____ may serve as an instrument for entrepreneurial activities for the university and engage in such activities as purchasing, developing, or managing real estate for university expansion, student housing, or retirement communities. It also may hold licensing agreements and other forms of intellectual property, borrow or guarantee debt issued by their parties, or engage in other activities to increase foundation revenue with no direct connection to a university purpose.

- When distributing gift funds to the university, the _____ will disclose any terms, conditions, or limitations imposed by donor or legal determination on the gift. The _____will abide by such restrictions and provide appropriate documentation.

Transfer of Funds

- The_____ is the primary depository of private gifts and will transfer funds to the designated entity within the institution in compliance with applicable laws, university policies, and gift agreements.

- The_____'s disbursements on behalf of the university must be reasonable business expenses that support the institution, are consistent with donor intent, and do not conflict with the law.

Foundation Funding and Administration

- The _____ is responsible for establishing a financial plan to underwrite the cost of foundation programs, operations, and services.

- The _____ has the right to use a reasonable percentage of the annual unrestricted funds, assess fees for services, or impose gift taxes, to support its operations. [Note: The use of fees and taxes should be disclosed to donors and institution staff.]

- The _____ , at its own expense, will provide office space, computer and telephone systems, utilities, adequate personnel, office supplies, and other such services that may be necessary or required to fulfill its responsibilities and obligations. *[Note: Depending on the degree of independence of the foundation, and if state law permits, the institution may help the foundation by providing support that may include personnel, office space, utilities, and services, or it may contract with the foundation for the services it provides; language should take this into account. Language should also be added to clarify whether the institution or the foundation owns the computer server and the records on the server. Institution gifts-in-kind will be appropriately reported in the foundation's annual report.]*

- The _____ shall maintain, at its own expense, copies of the plans, budgets, and donor and alumni records developed in connection with the performance of its obligations.

- The _____ will provide access to data and records to the university on a need-to-know basis in accordance with applicable laws, foundation policies, and guidelines. The foundation will provide copies of its annual report, and other information that may be publicly released.

Terms of the Memorandum of Understanding (MOU)

This Memorandum of Understanding, made this ___ of _____ , 20__ , by and between the board of the _____ and the _____ (an Internal Revenue Code §501 (c) (3) nonprofit corporation), is intended to set forth policies and procedures that will contribute to the coordination of their mutual activities.

To ensure effective achievement of the items of the agreement, the university and foundation officers and board representatives shall hold periodic meetings to foster and maintain productive relationships and to ensure open and continuing communications and alignment of priorities.

Either party may, upon 90 days prior written notice to the other, terminate this agreement. Notwithstanding the foregoing, either party may terminate this MOU in the event the other party defaults in the performance of its obligations and fails to cure the default within a reasonable time after receiving written show cause notice.

Should the university choose to terminate this agreement the foundation may require the university to pay, within 180 days of written notice, all debt incurred by the foundation on the university's behalf including, but not limited to, lease payments, advanced funds, and funds borrowed for specific initiatives. Should the foundation choose to terminate this agreement the university may require the foundation to pay debt it holds on behalf of the foundation in like manner.

Consistent with provisions appearing in the foundation's bylaws and its articles of incorporation, should the foundation cease to exist or cease to be an Internal Revenue Code §501(c)(3) organization, the foundation will transfer its assets and property to the institution, to the university, to a reincorporated successor foundation, or to the state or federal government for public purposes, in accordance with the law and donor intent.

IN WITNESS WHEREOF, the parties have caused this Memorandum of Understanding to be executed by their duly authorized officers as of the day and date first above written.

_____
Chair
Board of [name of institution or system]
Date:

_____
Chair
Board of [name of foundation]
Date:

_____
Chief Executive
[Name of institution or system]
Date:

_____
Chief Executive
[Name of foundation]
Date:

Appendix D

Illustrative Investment Policy
for Public Institutionally Related Foundations

Statement of Investment Policy for the XYZ Foundation

Contents:

1. Definition and Function

In recognition of its fiduciary responsibilities, the Board of Directors of the XYZ Foundation has adopted the following statement of investment policy. These guidelines relate to those gifts and donations in the form of endowments, with long-term benefit objectives; those funds set aside and designated by the board as quasi-endowment, and to those contributions received for the current benefit of the institution.

Investments generally will be limited to those firms and/or securities that adhere to the standards of these guidelines and meet prudent investment standards.

2. Statement of Purpose

The purpose of the endowment is to provide support for [name of higher education institution or system] and its mission over the long term. Accordingly, the purpose of this statement is to establish a written procedure for the investment of this foundation's endowment assets and to ensure that the future growth of these assets is sufficient to offset normal inflation plus reasonable spending, thereby preserving the constant dollar value and purchasing power of the endowment for future generations. Additionally, this statement will outline the guidelines meant to preserve the principal of operating cash and reserves while producing market-level income. This statement will establish appropriate risk and return objectives in light of the endowment's risk tolerance and investment time horizon. These objectives, as well as asset-allocation guidelines, suitable investments, and responsibilities of investment managers, are outlined below.

3. Objectives of the Endowment

The objectives of the endowment shall be defined as follows: *Absolute,* which shall be measured in real (net of inflation) rate-of-return terms and shall have the longest time horizon for measurement; *relative*, which shall be measured as time-weighted rates of return versus capital market indices; and *comparative*, which shall be measured as the performance of the investment managers compared with a universe of similar investment funds.

The absolute objective of the endowment is to seek an average total annual real return of 5 percent, or CPI plus 5 percent. This objective shall be measured over an annualized, rolling five-year and ten-year time period; the intent of this objective is to preserve, over time, the principal value of assets as measured in real, inflation-adjusted terms.

The relative objective of the endowment is to seek competitive investment performance versus appropriate capital market measures, such as securities indices. This objective shall be measured primarily by comparing investment results, over a moving annualized three-year and five-year time period, to the following:

- the Standard and Poor's 500 Index as a benchmark for the equity component;

- the Lehman Aggregate Bond Index as a benchmark for the fixed-income component; and

- the 90-day Treasury Bill Index as the benchmark for the cash and equivalent component.

The comparative performance objective of the endowment is to achieve a total rate of return that is above the median performance of the universe of similarly managed funds.

The endowment and quasi-endowment assets have a long-term, indefinite time horizon that runs concurrent with the endurance of the institution, in perpetuity. As such, these funds can assume a time horizon that extends well beyond a normal market cycle and can assume an above-average level of risk as measured by the standard deviation of annual returns. It is expected, however, that both professional management and sufficient portfolio diversification will smooth volatility and help to ensure a reasonable consistency of return.

4. Target Asset Allocation

To achieve its investment objectives, the endowment shall be allocated among a number of asset classes. These asset classes may include domestic equity, domestic fixed income, international equity, international fixed income, real estate, venture capital, private equity, hedge funds, commodities, and cash. The purpose of allocating among asset classes is to ensure the proper level of diversification within the endowment.

The following target asset-mix table defines the endowment's target asset allocation and the minimum and maximum allocation limits of each asset class:

Target Asset-Mix Table

Asset Class	Minimum Weight	Target Weight	Maximum Weight	Representative Index
Equities	XX%	XX%	XX%	S&P 500/others
Fixed Income	XX%	XX%	XX%	Lehman Aggregate
Alternative Investments	XX%	XX%	XX%	Various
Cash & Equivalents	XX%	XX%	XX%	90 Day T-bills
Other Securities	XX%	XX%	XX%	Other Index

The investment returns achieved by the investment managers will be compared with the investment returns achieved by a target portfolio. The target portfolio will consist of the weighted returns of the target asset mix: XX percent of the S&P 500 Index, XX percent of the Lehman Aggregate Bond Index, XX percent of the 90-day T-Bill Index, and XX percent of the other indices.

The general policy shall be to diversify investments among both equity and fixed-income securities so as to provide a balance that will enhance total return while avoiding undue risk concentration in any single asset class or investment category.

5. Investment Policies, Guidelines, and Restrictions

The investment polices, guidelines, and restrictions presented in this policy statement serve as a framework to help the endowment and its investment managers achieve the investment objectives at an acceptable level of risk. The endowment will be diversified both by asset class and within asset classes. Within each asset class, securities will be diversified among economic sector, industry, quality, and size. The purpose of diversification is to provide reasonable assurance that no single security or class of securities will have a disproportionate impact on the performance of the total fund. As a result, the risk level associated with the portfolio investment is reduced.

Within the equity and fixed-income asset classes, managers with different investment styles and emphasizing various capitalization ranges will be employed. Diversification by investment style is also an important step in reducing the risk of the portfolio.

Equity Securities. The purpose of equity investments, both domestic and international, in the endowment is to provide capital appreciation and growth of income with the recognition that this asset class carries with it the assumption of greater market volatility and increased risk of loss. The investment managers should maintain the equity portion of the portfolio at a risk level roughly equivalent to that of the equity market as a whole, with an additional objective of exceeding its results as represented by the annualized returns of the S&P 500 Index, over an annualized moving three-year and five-year time period.

Investment styles within the equity asset class are defined as follows:

- **Core Equity** — equity securities whose portfolio characteristics are similar to that of the S&P 500 Index, with the objectives of adding value over and above the index, typically from sector or issue selection.

- **Growth** — stocks of companies that are expected to have above-average prospects for long-term growth in earnings and profitability.

- **Value** — stocks of companies believed to be undervalued or possessing lower than average price-to-earnings ratios, based on their potential for capital appreciation.

- **Small Capitalization** — stocks of companies from the above styles, with relatively small market-value capitalization. (The average market capitalization is expected to be approximately $500 million.)

- **International** — stocks of companies domiciled outside of the United States.

Equity holdings generally shall be restricted to high-quality, readily marketable securities of corporations that are actively traded on the major stock exchanges, including Nasdaq. International equity investments of similar quality and marketability will be permitted up to X percent of the total equity portfolio.

Equity holdings generally must represent companies meeting a minimum market capitalization requirement of $100 million with reasonable market liquidity. Decisions as to individual security selection, number of industries and holdings, current income levels, and turnover are left to broad manager discretion, subject to the standards of fiduciary prudence. However, no single major industry shall represent more than 20 percent of the total market value of the endowment, and no single security shall represent more than 5 percent of the total market value of the endowment.

The investment managers are prohibited from selling securities short; buying securities on margin; borrowing money or pledging assets; or trading uncovered options, commodities, or currencies without the advance written approval of the foundation. The managers also are restricted from investing in private placements and restricted stock unless otherwise permitted in writing by the foundation. It is expected that no assets will be invested in securities whose issuers are or are reasonably expected to become insolvent or who otherwise have filed a petition under any state or federal bankruptcy or similar statute.

Within the above guidelines and restrictions, managers have complete discretion over the timing and selection of equity securities.

Fixed-Income Securities. Investments in fixed-income securities should be actively managed to pursue opportunities presented by changes in interest rates, sector allocations, and maturity premiums, with the objective of meeting or exceeding the results of the fixed-income market as represented by the annualized returns of the Lehman Aggregate Bond Index over an annualized moving three-year and five-year time period.

The investment managers may invest in obligations of the U.S. government and its agencies, corporate debt securities, mortgage-backed, and asset-backed securities. These investments will be subject to the following limitations:

* No issues may be purchased with more than 30 years to maturity;

* Investments of a single issuer, with the exception of the U.S. government and its agencies (including GNMA, FNMA, and FHLMC), may not exceed 5 percent of the total market value of the portfolio;

* No more than 15 percent of the corporate debt securities in the fixed-income portfolio may be rated below investment grade; and

* No more than 10 percent of the fixed-income portfolio may be invested in non-U.S.-denominated securities.

Within the fixed-income component, the investment managers are prohibited from investing in private placements and fixed-income or interest rate futures without the prior written approval of the foundation. Within the above guidelines and restrictions, the managers have complete discretion over the timing and selection of fixed-income securities.

Alternative Investments. Marketable alternative investments are broadly defined to include hedge funds, absolute return and special situation funds, distressed debt, market neutral, and other nontraditional investment strategies whose underlying securities are traded on public exchanges or are otherwise readily marketable. Alternative marketable investments may be made by the endowment directly or through partnerships. Funds of funds may be utilized as long as the total fees paid are reasonable and within industry ranges. The breadth of hedge-fund strategies is very broad, and the selection of appropriate investments in this area must be made with the help of knowledgeable and experienced people in the field. The committee should assess the risk-and-return guidelines of each strategy in light of the role of that strategy in the total portfolio of hedge funds. In no case should any one hedge fund account for more than 2 percent of the market value of the total endowment.

Alternative nonmarketable investments are expected to earn superior equity-type returns over extended periods in order to justify their illiquid (lockup) status. The advantages of nonmarketable investments include their ability to enhance long-term returns through investment in inefficient, complex markets. They offer reduced volatility of asset values by offering low correlation with listed securities and fixed-income instruments. The disadvantage of the asset class is its illiquidity and more complex fee structures, and performance frequently is dependent on the quality of external managers. The foundation expects to control the risks of alternative nonmarketable investments through extensive due diligence and diversification. These investments may be held directly or through limited partnerships. Typically, they include venture capital, private equity, international venture capital, private equity, real estate, mezzanine debt, and energy, commodities, and natural resources.

Venture Capital and Other Private Equity Partnerships. Investments may also include venture capital and private equity investments, held in the form of professionally managed pooled limited partnership investments. Such investments shall not exceed X percent of total endowment assets, and must be made through funds offered by professional investment managers with proven records of superior performance over time.

- *Real Estate* — investments held in the form of professionally managed, income-producing commercial and residential property. Such investments may not exceed X percent of the total endowment fund and may be made only through professionally managed pooled real estate investment funds, as offered by leading real estate managers with proven records of superior performance over time.

  Gifts of income-producing real estate may be included temporarily in the endowment portfolio and liquidated at the earliest convenient time, while donors of gift real estate intended for institutional use and occupancy on a permanent basis should be discouraged from making the contribution as endowment. To the extent any gifts of real estate would constitute a negative cash flow or would be deemed by professional management counsel to constitute undue market risk, such gifts would be disposed at sale and the

155

proceeds directed to the general endowment pool for the benefit of programs consistent with the donor's interest.

- *Derivatives and Derivative Securities* — shall be discouraged, unless such an opportunity presents itself that the use of these sophisticated securities would provide substantial opportunity to increase investment returns or lower investment costs at an appropriately equivalent level of risk to the remainder of the total portfolio. The approval and use of derivative securities will not be allowed unless the foundation is confident that the investment manager(s) thoroughly understands the risks being taken, has demonstrated expertise in their usage of such securities, and has guidelines in place for the use and monitoring of derivatives.

Cash and Equivalents. The investment manager may invest in the highest quality commercial paper, repurchase agreements, Treasury bills, certificates of deposit, and money-market funds to provide income, liquidity for expense payments, and preservation of the endowment's principal value. Commercial paper assets must be rated at least A-1 or P-1 (by Moody's or S&P). No more than 5 percent of the total market value of the endowment's assets may be invested in the obligations of a single issuer, with the exception of the U.S. government and its agencies.

Uninvested cash reserves shall be kept to a minimum; short-term cash-equivalent securities usually are not considered an appropriate investment vehicle for endowment assets. However, such vehicles are appropriate as depository for income distributions from longer term endowment investments or as needed for temporary placement of funds directed for future investment to the longer term capital markets. Also, such investments are the standard for contributions to the current fund or for current operating cash.

Within the above guidelines and restrictions, the managers have complete discretion over the timing and selection of cash-equivalent securities.

Restrictions. The investment committee is authorized to waive or modify any of the restrictions in these guidelines in appropriate circumstances. Any such waiver or modification will be made only after a thorough review of the manager and the investment strategy involved. Documentation supporting all waivers and modifications will be maintained as part of the permanent records of the investment committee. All waivers and modifications will be reported to the board of directors at the meeting immediately following the granting of the waiver or modification.

6. Communications

The investment managers shall meet regularly, or as reasonably expected, with the foundation investment committee. Investment policy shall be reviewed during such meetings and no less than annually.

Manager Reporting and Evaluation. It is expected that the investment managers responsible for the investment of foundation assets shall report quarterly to the committee on the performance of the portfolio, including comparative gross returns for the funds and their respective benchmarks. Also included will be a complete accounting of all transactions involving the endowment during the quarter, together with a statement of beginning market value, fees, capital appreciation, income, and ending market value, for each account.

The foundation recognizes that market conditions may greatly influence the ability of a manager to meet year-to-year investment goals and objectives. Further, the foundation realizes that significant cash flow also may affect the ability of a manager to meet a specific short-term objective. Accordingly, the foundation expects to monitor performance through absolute, relative, and comparative terms over annualized time periods. Absolute results will determine the rate of fund growth, while relative results will provide the foundation with a view of investment performance compared with the securities markets, and comparative results will present performance compared with other investment managers.

Review of portfolio results in *absolute* terms shall be made with consideration towards meeting and/or exceeding the expressed minimum real rate of return over a moving five-year and ten-year time period.

Review of portfolio results in *relative* terms shall be accomplished primarily by comparing results over a moving annualized three-year and five-year time periods to assigned market indices.

Review of portfolio results in *comparative* terms shall be accomplished primarily through universe comparisons over moving annualized one-year, three-year, and/or five-year time periods.

Spending Policy. It is the foundation's policy to distribute annually X percent of a trailing three-year or five-year average of the endowment's total asset value, with the understanding that this spending rate plus inflation will not normally exceed total return from investment. However, it is understood that this total return basis for calculating spending is sanctioned by the Uniform Management of Institutional Funds Act (UMIFA), under which guidelines the foundation is permitted to spend an amount in excess of the current yield (interest and dividends earned), including realized or unrealized appreciation.

Rebalancing Policy. It is the foundation's policy to rebalance to its target asset allocation on a uniform basis so as not to cause undue expense to be allocated to the portfolio. It is the foundation's policy to have the committee review rebalancing of the portfolio at least annually — or sooner, if desired by the members of the committee. The method of rebalancing will be based upon the "tolerance" rebalancing formula, which generally states that the portfolio will be rebalanced if the target asset allocation moves beyond the stated tolerance for any particular asset category. As an example, if the target asset allocation for equities is 65 percent with a 5 percent tolerance, than no rebalancing would be required under this investment policy if the range for equity investments remained within a 60 percent to 70 percent range; otherwise, management is required to direct investment advisers to rebalance once the limits are achieved. Further, at least annually (usually the date of the annual review with investment managers by the committee) the portfolio will be rebalanced regardless of its stated allocation to asset classes.

Acknowledgment

This statement of investment policy is accepted and entered into by the foundation and the investment managers. Any revisions or changes in policy shall be made in writing and accepted by both parties.

Any changes within the management firm — ownership, principals, specific portfolio managers, or changes in investment philosophy — should be communicated as soon as possible to the foundation and its representatives.

ACCEPTED: _____ Date _____
      XYZ Foundation

ACCEPTED: _____ Date _____
      Investment Manager

Appendix E

Illustrative Gift Acceptance Policy[†]

Purpose of the Policy

This policy establishes guidelines to be followed by the XYZ Foundation (foundation) in the solicitation, acceptance, and utilization of gifts in support of the XYZ university or system. The policy addresses ethical practices, authority to negotiate and accept gifts, donor recognition, gift restrictions, endowment agreements, accounting and investment guidelines, and acceptance of outright and planned gifts by the foundation.

The policy outlines the administrative, legal, and accounting practices and procedures to be followed in order to ensure that consistent and equitable relations are maintained with donors.

Specifically, the XYZ Foundation will adhere to the following tenets:

Standards of Ethical Practice

It is the policy of the foundation to encourage, inform, and assist donors who wish to support the mission and priorities of XYZ university or system, but never to pressure or attempt to unduly persuade prospective donors. Persons acting on behalf of the foundation will do so with fairness, honesty, integrity, ethics, and openness.

The foundation will not provide legal or tax advice to donors. Individuals acting on behalf of the foundation may provide general legal and tax information obtained from reliable qualified sources to prospective donors, but they should advise donors to consult with competent professional advisors with respect to the legal and tax implications of gifts.

The foundation will not accept any gifts that in the opinion of the foundation chief executive or the board's development committee may jeopardize the foundation's tax-exempt status.

[†] AGB extends special thanks to the New Mexico State University foundation for granting permission for adaptation of its comprehensive policy.

- Persons acting on behalf of the foundation will fully disclose the role and relationship of each party involved in the planning or negotiation of gifts to the foundation.

- Licensed professionals affiliated with the foundation may represent donors for any proposed gift to the foundation only after full disclosure is made to the donor of such affiliation.

- Individuals acting on behalf of the foundation may not receive financial benefit from any gift to the foundation, except for salaries to employees of the foundation and standard and reasonable fees to licensed professionals. Finders' fees and commissions will not be paid to persons engaged to contact or cultivate prospective donors or to promote gifts to the foundation.

- Except as required by law, all information obtained from or about donors or prospective donors will be held in strict confidence by the foundation and may be shared among foundation staff members and board development committee members only to the extent required to carry out their duties and responsibilities. Specific requests from donors for confidentiality or anonymity will always be honored.

- The foundation will not serve as personal representative, executor, or administrator of any estate, or trustee of any trust, in which it is not the sole beneficiary.

- The foundation will not accept gifts from any donor that stipulate the designation of a specific recipient (for example, a scholarship recipient).

Authority to Negotiate, Accept, Decline, or Disclaim Gifts

The chief executive of the foundation has the authority to accept gifts made to the foundation (or the university or system) in accordance with the provisions of this policy, which in the opinion of the chief executive of the foundation will assist the foundation in carrying out its mission and goals. The foundation chief executive may decline or disclaim any gift that is (1) considered to be inappropriate, (2) would not serve the purposes of the foundation (or that of the university or system), or (3) the acceptance of which would be contrary to the provisions of this policy or other policies of the foundation, or contrary to any policy of the university or system.

The chief executive of the foundation is responsible for the development, maintenance, and oversight of procedures for the execution and adherence to the provisions of this gift acceptance policy.

The chief executive of the foundation may engage other professionals in order to make a judgment regarding the acceptance, decline, or disclaimer of any gift. The chief executive may refer any decision with respect to the acceptance, decline, or disclaimer of any gift to the appropriate committee (development committee) of the foundation.

The chief executive of the foundation may delegate these authorities to any employee of the foundation, provided such delegation be reported to the foundation's development committee or other appropriate committee.

161

Recognition of Donors

Donors will be advised at the time of each gift that the foundation will publicly recognize donors, unless requested otherwise by the donor. Requests declining public recognition will be documented and retained in the permanent files of the foundation.

Recognition of donors will be made on the basis of the value of the gift(s) made to the foundation. The specific value of individual gifts will not be disclosed publicly, unless agreed to in writing by the donor and the foundation. The value of gifts for public recognition will be categorized by ranges of value as determined by the chief executive of the foundation with the advice and consent of the development committee according to the following guidelines:

- Only irrevocable gifts will be recognized.

- Gifts will be recognized at values eligible for a charitable deduction from income for federal income-tax purposes.

- Recognition that includes the naming of a facility, college, school, department, program, faculty chair, professorship, fellowship or other specific naming opportunity in honor of a donor will be made in accordance with the naming procedures of the institution or system.

- Written receipts will be provided to donors in a sufficiently timely manner to enable donors to comply with IRS regulations requiring charitable gift receipt documentation.

Gift Restrictions and Limitations of Use

The foundation will honor the donor's intent with respect to the use of any gift that does not conflict with the foundation and the university or system's mission, provided the intent can be honored within the capabilities of university/system faculty and staff, facilities, and finances.

The foundation will accept gifts of tangible assets that are readily marketable and/or converted into cash at the discretion of the foundation in order to provide the greatest amount of flexibility in meeting the mission of the foundation, university, or system. Approval of the foundation's development committee is required to accept any gift of tangible assets with conditions requiring retention, unusual restrictions, or unusual limitations. If the donor intends to impose such conditions on a gift, prior approval by the president or chancellor of the university or system is required.

Endowment and Gift Limitation Agreements

The terms and conditions of all gifts to the foundation on which the donor has placed limitations (the use of the gift or restrictions on distributions of the gift) must be documented in writing and signed by the donor and authorized by a representative of the foundation.

Endowed gifts will be invested in the foundation's endowment fund and governed by the foundation's investment and spending policies. Endowed gift agreements will also acknowledge that the donor has made the gift subject to the provisions of the foundation's gift acceptance policy. Agreements that do not reflect these provisions must be approved by the foundation's development committee.

No distribution will be made from an endowment fund in which the total contributions and additions to the fund are less than the minimum endowment amount when the endowment was established. Earnings allocated to an endowment fund will be allocated to the corpus of the endowment fund, under the circumstances stated above.

Accounting and Investment Standards

The foundation will maintain accounting records that are consistent with the standards set forth by the Financial Accounting Standards Board (FASB), the Prudent Investor Act (PIA), and the Uniform Management of Institutional Funds Act (UMIFA), as revised from time to time.

Guidelines for Acceptance of Outright Gifts

The foundation has the authority to accept outright gifts (those in which complete title of the gifted property vests immediately with the foundation), including those gifts on which the donor has placed restrictions on distributions from the gift or limitations on the use of the gift.

If the foundation elects to pay a part of all of the costs associated with the transfer of gifts from donors or the sale of assets, such costs will be paid from the gift or on the proceeds of the sale of the gift, not from the general assets of the foundation.

The XYZ Foundation will accept the following outright gifts:

1. Cash and Publicly Traded, Marketable Securities

Gifts of cash and publicly traded, marketable securities that can be converted to cash by sale on recognized security exchanges may be accepted without limitation by the foundation. These gifts will be valued for gift purposes in accordance with IRS procedures in effect for the determinations of charitable income-tax deductions.

2. Non-publicly Traded Securities

Gifts of stock in non-publicly traded corporations or limited liability companies, and interest in limited partnerships or joint ventures may be accepted only if the foundation determines that the asset can be sold within a reasonable period of time and is in the best interest of the foundation or the university or system.

The foundation will not accept any interest in general partnerships or other business entities in which the foundation may be liable for debts, judgments, or other liabilities incurred by the business entity. The foundation will generally not accept a gift of a non-publicly traded security for which the foundation may become responsible for the management of the entity that has issued the security.

Because of the specific knowledge required for each gift of non-publicly traded securities, the development committee will set an appropriate minimum dollar amount deemed acceptable by the foundation. An appraisal by an independent qualified appraiser that meets the standards established by the IRS for deduction as a charitable contribution will be provided to the foundation. The donor will pay the cost of the appraisal unless the foundation agrees to pay part or all of the cost based on the relative value of the gift.

3. Real Estate

The foundation will accept gifts of real estate, including fractional interests, assignments of leases, leasehold interests, mineral rights, royalty interests, or other rights severed from the fee title. Because of the time and cost associated with administering and managing real property, the development committee should set a minimum dollar value deemed acceptable by the foundation.

Upon notification of a prospective donor's potential contribution of real estate, the chief executive of the foundation, or a member of the foundation's development or real estate committees, or other persons acting on the foundation's behalf, will make an on-site inspection of the property to make a preliminary assessment of the property based on the following:

- The property meets the minimum dollar market value set by the appropriate committee of the foundation board;

- There is no apparent environmental contamination that would require remediation by the foundation;

- There is apparent legal ingress and egress;

- The property may reasonably be expected to be marketable in one year or less; and

- The property may likely be administered and managed by the foundation or its agents at costs commensurate with the value and income that may be derived from the property during any period of time the foundation may hold it.

A written report of the inspection and findings will be retained in the foundation's files.

Prior to acceptance of the gift, the following will be provided to the foundation:

- Appraisal by an independent appraiser licensed in the state in which the property is located that meets the standards to support a charitable deduction for the gift, as prescribed by the IRS.

- A Phase I environmental assessment prepared by an independent firm licensed in the state where the property is located that reflects any environmental contamination for which the Environmental Protection Agency or state or local governing authority would require remediation.

- Verification that all liens and encumbrances are satisfied and title defects corrected prior to acceptance of title by the foundation, and a commitment for an owner's title insurance policy issued by a title insurance company licensed in the state where the property is located.

Costs associated with obtaining the above documents will be the responsibility of the prospective donor, unless the foundation agrees to pay part or all of the costs based on the value of the real estate to be given.

4. Non-publicly Traded, Closely Held Business Interests

The foundation will not accept gifts of non-publicly traded closely held business interests unless the foundation determines that the business interest should be retained as an asset of the foundation. The development committee of the foundation must approve all such gifts.

5. Tangible Personal Property

Gifts of tangible personal property acceptable to the foundation include gifts that the donor possesses or has the right to sell, give, or otherwise dispose of. Types of personal property gifts include, but are not limited to, works of art, taxidermy, stamp and coin collections, manuscripts, literary works, boats, motor vehicles, machinery, equipment, furniture, jewelry, computer hardware and software (only after a review indicates that the property is either readily marketable or needed by the university or system in a manner that is related to education, research, or a combination thereof). The foundation will accept gifts of personal property only if (1) the property is free of liens and encumbrances; (2) its physical condition is satisfactory to the foundation; (3) it can be sold within a reasonable period of time; (4) the costs of relocating the property to the foundation's possession are commensurate with its value; and (5) the value of the asset has been established in writing by an independent appraiser or expert with knowledge of the current market for that asset.

6. Life Insurance Policies

The foundation may accept gifts of life insurance policies by a transfer of ownership from the owner of the policy to the foundation. The policy will be valued at the value recognized by the IRS for a charitable gift deduction at the time of transfer to the foundation. The foundation may exercise the rights of ownership of the policy at any time, including continuation of premiums on the policy if not a paid-up policy, redemption of the policy, conversion to a paid-up policy, conversion to an extended term policy, or any other ownership right under the policy. If the donor has expressed intent to pay future premiums due on the policy, such intent will be obtained in writing, and contributions for future premiums will be paid to the foundation and remitted by the foundation to the insurance company. Contributions from the donor for premium payments will be recognized as cash contributions to the foundation at the time received by the foundation.

A donor may designate the foundation as a beneficiary or contingent beneficiary of a life insurance policy. The gift should be recognized at the time and in the amount of the benefit when paid to the foundation.

7. Gifts of Other Assets

Gifts of assets for which guidelines have not been provided in this policy may be accepted with approval of the development committee of the foundation.

Guidelines for Acceptance of Other Planned Gifts

The foundation will accept planned gifts or any gift made by a donor by will, trust, or other legal instrument in which title to the property does not vest immediately in the foundation. Such gifts may be revocable or irrevocable.

Irrevocable gifts will be recognized at values established and recognized under IRS regulations for charitable gifts for federal income-tax deductions. Revocable planned gifts will be recognized at the time the property passes to the foundation.

Planned gifts generally acceptable by the foundation include charitable bequests, retirement plans, charitable gift annuities, charitable remainder trusts, charitable lead trusts, remainder interests subject to life estates, and pay-on-death accounts.

- Charitable bequests and retirement plans. Donors can make charitable bequests to the foundation in wills or living trusts, or they can name the foundation as beneficiary of their retirement plans.

- Charitable gift annuities. The foundation will accept contracts that are signed between the foundation and the donor where foundation assets back the income payments of a gift annuity contract. The annual payment to the annuitant is based on the donor's age and the fair market value of the contribution made by the donor even though the actual gift to the foundation has a value less than the donor's contribution. The foundation will pay gift annuity rates as recommended by the American Council on Gift Annuities.

- Charitable remainder trusts, including annuity trusts and unitrusts. The foundation will accept annuity trusts where the donor and/or beneficiary annually receives a payout that is fixed irrevocably at the time of the gift and stated in a trust agreement. The payout by the foundation will be equal to 5 percent (or a percentage set by the foundation's development committee) of the fair market value of the assets placed in the trust when it is created. Income in excess of the annual payment is added to the principal. The foundation will accept unitrusts, which provide for payment to the donor and/or beneficiary an amount equal to a set percentage of fair market value of the assets of the trust, valued annually. The percentage is determined at the time the trust is created, is stated in the trust, and is permanent. The minimum payout by the foundation will be 5 percent annually (or a percentage set by the foundation's development committee).

- Charitable lead trusts. The foundation will accept lead trusts or gifts designed to generate periodic payments to the foundation for a period of several years, after which the trust terminates and the assets pass to the designated individuals either outright or in trust.

- Remainder interest subject to life estate. The foundation will accept gifts of a personal residence or farm while the donor retains a life estate, and the foundation receives the remainder interest.

The guidelines for acceptance of gifts as set forth in this policy will be applicable to assets received through planned gift instruments. If representatives of the foundation participate in the process of establishing a planned gift, the donor will be advised of applicable policy provisions so that the planned gift documents will conform to this policy. In instances in which the foundation has no knowledge of the planned gift until the terminating event occurs, consideration will be given to disclaiming any asset that does not conform to this policy.

The foundation will advise prospective donors that they should engage professional representation and that costs associated with the preparation of all required legal documents must be paid by the donor in order to ensure that the interests of the donor are fully represented by counsel.

All costs associated with the administration of and distribution from a planned gift instrument, except for gift annuities administered by the foundation, will be paid from the assets or income of the trust, estate, or other applicable legal arrangement used for the planned gift. If the planned gift to the foundation includes provisions for the establishment of an endowment fund transfer to

167

an existing endowment fund, or other limitations on the use of the gift, the foundation may use the gift assets to cover any costs.

Amendments to and Interpretations of Policy

This policy may be amended or repealed — at a meeting of the board of directors of the foundation in which a quorum of the voting members are present — by a two-thirds vote of voting members present.

Adopted on _____ by the board of directors of the _____ foundation.

_____   _____
Chief Executive   Board Chair
XYZ Foundation   *XYZ Foundation*

Margin of Excellence
THE NEW WORK OF HIGHER EDUCATION FOUNDATIONS

ABOUT THE AUTHORS

About the Authors

Larry S. Boulet is chairman of the Indiana State University Foundation and serves as a board member and chairman of the audit committee of a publicly traded company. He is a former senior audit partner with the international accounting firm of PricewaterhouseCoopers and is the president of Boulet Consulting, LLC, a firm specializing in merger and acquisition transactions and matters of corporate governance.

Gerald B. Fischer has been president and chief executive officer of the University of Minnesota Foundation since 1990. His career includes nearly 20 years with Ford Motor Company and affiliated companies, where he held several positions in the finance offices of Ford, Ford Credit, and Ford of Europe. In 1985, he became senior vice president-finance for First Bank System (now U.S. Bancorp) in Minneapolis and was appointed executive vice president, chief financial officer, and treasurer in 1986. Fischer is a director of SurModics, Inc., and serves on the boards of the University Gateway Corporation and UMIFA. He is also on two national AGF advisory panels. Fischer is board chair of the Interlochen Center for the Arts in Interlochen, Mich., and a former trustee of the College of Wooster and the Dale Warland Singers.

John F. Gallagher is vice president for development at the University of Nevada, Las Vegas (UNLV), a position he has held since May 1995, and the executive director of the UNLV Foundation. In these roles, he serves as the university's chief development officer, leads all of UNLV's fund-raising programs, and oversees the active management of about $200 million in assets for the benefit of the university's students and faculty. Prior to UNLV, Gallagher was vice president for university relations at the University of Puget Sound in Tacoma, Wash. In a 30-year career in higher education, he also has worked at Seattle University, Evergreen State College, St. Martin's College, and the University of Washington. Gallagher is a member of the board of directors of the Council for the Advancement and Support of Education (CASE) District VII-Far West.

John S. Griswold, Jr. is senior vice president, marketing services and external relations of Commonfund Group and oversees all internal and external communications for Commonfund, including media and public relations. Griswold also serves as executive director of the Commonfund Institute. In this capacity, he directs Commonfund's educational, market research, and professional development activities and initiates and supervises Commonfund's Benchmarks

Studies of educational endowments, foundations, and health-care institutions. Griswold has written several articles and book chapters on endowment management and the management of investment committees. He is a member of numerous nonprofit boards and investment committees, including the Pomfret School in Connecticut, the Regional Plan Association, the Colony Foundation, and the Boys and Girls Clubs of America.

Carol C. Harter is president of the University of Nevada, Las Vegas (UNLV), a post she has held for the past ten years. During her tenure, she has advanced UNLV to major research university status and has overseen the significant enhancement of private and research funding. Prior to her arrival at UNLV, Harter served as president of the State University of New York at Geneseo for six years and spent almost 19 years at Ohio University, where she was a faculty member and ombudsman, and where she served in two vice presidencies. She is the author of numerous journal articles and published papers in English literature and higher education and has co-authored two books on American writers.

Royster C. Hedgepeth is principal consultant and chief executive officer of the Hedgepeth Group, an organizational development firm serving colleges and universities and their related foundations, independent schools, and a variety of education, arts, religious, and social organizations. Prior to founding CWC/Hedgepeth Group, Hedgepeth had 26 years of educational fund-raising experience, including directing extremely successful first-time campaigns for the universities of Illinois, Colorado, and Massachusetts. Hedgepeth is the author of *How Public College and University Foundation Boards Contribute to Campaign Success*, published by AGB.

Kevin Hoolehan is managing director of the Indiana State University Foundation, where he has initiated numerous changes in finance, process, communication, and control and has managed the transition of the organization to a large, modern foundation. Before that he was a banker, restaurateur, publishing executive, fund-raiser, and a state department of revenue official. Hoolehan has served on a number of boards and commissions in Indiana.

Richard T. Ingram is president of the AGB, having previously served as executive vice president. He has served on several governing boards, including those of two private colleges, an independent preparatory school, and an insurance company. Ingram has written extensively on trusteeship matters for such publications as *Educational Record*, the *Chronicle of Higher Education*, and AGB's *Trusteeship* magazine. His monographs and books include primers on the elements of effective trusteeship; a recent book on presidential and board assessment; pamphlets on board organization, bylaws, and structure; and trustee conflict-of-interest policies.

James L. Lanier, Jr., emeritus president of the East Carolina University Foundation, Inc. and the ECU Real Estate Foundation, Inc., also served for 20 years as vice chancellor for institutional advancement and chief executive officer of the foundations. Lanier currently serves on the boards of the Greenville Industries Corporation, the Harold H. Bate Foundation, and the Wesley Foundation of East Carolina, as well as on AGB's Advisory Council for Institutionally Related Foundations. Lanier chaired the joint AGB-CASE task force that developed the Illustrative Memorandum of Understanding between Universities and Foundations that appears in this book. In addition to serving as a CASE director for District III, he chaired the CASE National Assembly in 1997 and has served on numerous CASE commissions, including the national commission on philanthropy, the national commission on educational fund-raising, and the national marketing committee. He is a founding member and current chair of the CASE Board's National Steering Committee for Institutionally Related Foundations. In 2004, he was awarded the CASE-Commonfund Institutionally Related Foundation Professional Leadership Award.

173

Richard D. Legon is executive vice president of AGB. He becomes the president in January 2006. Legon's experience working with boards in higher education and in other areas of the nonprofit world spans more than 25 years, much of it focused on the board's responsibilities in the areas of fund-raising and finance. Legon frequently works with college, university, and foundation boards to address board responsibilities, board structure and development, and fund-raising effectiveness. He has been instrumental in developing AGB's portfolio of services for public college and university foundations. Legon has written several articles on the board's role in fund-raising for *Trusteeship* magazine and CASE *Currents* as well as two AGB Board Basics, "Governing Board and Foundation Board Relations," and "The Board's Role in Fund-Raising."

Marcia G. Muller came to Wright State University as vice president for university advancement and president of the Wright State University Foundation in July 1999, after nine years at New Mexico State University in similar capacities. Prior to that, she was vice president for external affairs at Long Island University in New York. In all, Muller has devoted more than 29 years to development and public relations, including four years as assistant vice president for development at the University of Miami and five years at the University of California, Irvine. At UC Irvine, Muller was first director of development at the College of Medicine and subsequently promoted assistant vice chancellor of university advancement for development with campuswide responsibilities. Muller has worked as grants coordinator for Girls Clubs of America, all in Southern California, and taught in the public schools of Deerfield and Wilmette, Ill.

Thomas Arden Roha is a partner in Roha & Flaherty, a Washington, D.C., law firm that represents nonprofit organizations, including colleges, universities, education associations, private foundations, and foundations affiliated with state institutions. Roha has spoken and written extensively on issues facing institutionally related foundations.

174

E.B. Wilson is chairman emeritus of St. Lawrence University in Canton, N.Y., where he served as a trustee for 16 years and chaired the committee on trustees, the academic and faculty affairs committee, the committee on institutional planning, the executive committee, and the compensation committee. Wilson also served for five years as a trustee of the Boston Conservatory and chaired the strategic planning committee, the academic affairs committee, and served on the executive committee, the committee on trustees, and the audit committee. He was chairman of the Executive Service Corps of New England from 1995-98. Wilson was a member of the AGB Council of Board Chairs and regularly contributes to *Trusteeship* magazine. He frequently serves as a facilitator for AGB programs on governance and trusteeship in higher education.

Index

180